The Mind Matters
Dr. Jerry M. Kelly

Foreword by Bishop Harold C. Ray

© Copyright 1998 — Jerry M. Kelly

All rights reserved. This book is protected under the copyright laws of the United States of America. This book may not be copied or reprinted for commercial gain or profit. The use of short quotations or occasional page copying for personal or group study is permitted and encouraged. Permission will be granted upon request. Unless otherwise identified, Scripture quotations are from the King James Version of the Bible.

Take note that the name satan and related names are not capitalized. We choose not to acknowledge him, even to the point of violating grammatical rules.

Treasure House

An Imprint of
**Destiny Image® Publishers, Inc.
P.O. Box 310
Shippensburg, PA 17257-0310**

"For where your treasure is,
there will your heart be also." Matthew 6:21

ISBN 1-56043-317-5

For Worldwide Distribution
Printed in the U.S.A.

First printing: 1998   Second printing: 2000

This book and all other Destiny Image, Revival Press, Mercy Place, Fresh Bread, and Treasure House books are available at Christian bookstores and distributors worldwide.

For a U.S. bookstore nearest you, call **1-800-722-6774**.
For more information on foreign distributors,
call **717-532-3040**.
Or reach us on the Internet: **http://www.reapernet.com**

DEDICATION

To the human mind.

To all who have given their hearts to Jesus.

To the one who finds life empty, aimless and void, but is seeking help for decision-making.

To you, the reader, for whom I desire to encourage and inspire to renew your mind by the Holy Spirit and activating the Word of God.

To all who are not clothed and in their right mind.

To every generation that seeks meaning and a reason for their minds being unsound.

To everyone who is seeking mind transformation.

ACKNOWLEDGMENTS

I am very appreciative toward the many members, friends, and colleagues at Antioch Christian Center Church in Petersburg, Virginia, whose faithfulness, prayers, and patience inspired me to compose such a "masterpiece" on a topic that is too often neglected, but is very critical for functioning in the kingdom of God in the 21st century.

For the construction and production of this book itself, I feel a deep sense of gratitude to the following:

My precious wife, Brenda, for her encouragement, inspiration, aiding in research, proofing and layout of this book.

Our son Larelle, daughter Jessica, and darling grandson Brandon, for their patience and support.

My mother, Irene P. Kelly, for her devotion to the Lord and to her children, for her constant demonstration of love that inspired me to pursue the maximization of my ability and potential.

In memory of my beloved father, Wilbur S. Kelly, and the legacy he left.

My father- and mother-in-law, James (Jimmy) and Lorraine Johnson, whose commitment to the work of our vision made this project possible.

Bishop Harold C. and Prophetess Brenda Ray, pastors of Redemptive Life Fellowship and presiding bishop of "The Kingdom Dominion Fellowship of Churches and Network" of West Palm Beach, Florida, for their fathering and mothering us through crucial times in ministry, as well as instructing us from a mentor's heart on things concerning the kingdom of God and economic empowerment.

Bishop Mack and Pastor Brenda Timberlake, Jr., pastors of Christian Faith Center and presiding bishop of Christian Faith Center Pastors and Ministers Fellowship of Creedmoor, North Carolina, for their shepherding and mentoring us in the Word of God, inspiring and motivating us in marriage, ministry and stability in life.

Special ACC members for their $1,000 contributions to aid in the cost of publishing this book: Ulysee and Carolyn Benson, Pauline Foster, Susan Hill, Fatina Little, Charles and Joyce Porter, Maurice and Laura Smith, Leander and Daisy Upperman, and Rickey and Ann Hall.

For contributions of $500 toward the publishing cost of this book: Lewis and Franco Downs, Gladys Pegeas, Leo and Sharon Petersen, James and Lorraine Johnson, and James and Lucille Young.

TABLE OF CONTENTS

Foreword..vii
Preface..ix
Introduction..xii

1. The Power of Mind Renewal...........................1
2. The Composites of a Sound Mind.................16
3. The Law of the Mind......................................24
4. The Readiness of the Mind............................32
5. The Nomadic Mindset...................................40
6. The Mind Matters I..48
7. The Mind Matters II.......................................56
8. The Mind Matters III......................................66
9. The Mind Matters IV.....................................73
10. Mind Over Matters...82
11. The Right and Wrong
    Way of Thinking..89
12. The Center Focus of
    Mind/State of Being....................................101
13. The Power of Thought.................................104
14. The Imagination of the Mind......................107
15. The Endurance of the Mind........................117

FOREWORD

As we stand on the threshold of an imaginative and innovative twenty-first century, filled with technological advances and almost unimaginable challenges for the building of our local communities, the summons issued to the born-again believer could not be more clarion. Indeed, over and over again communities of faith are proving their unique gifting and ability to overcome institutional and traditional forces of oppression and bondage, impacting and motivating individuals to recognize and embrace their prophetic destiny as a people of wealth, nobility and dignity.

The tragic irony of our times, however, is the fact that while God has raised up "shepherds after His own heart" who are indeed promulgating the full Gospel of Kingdom Dominion and exhorting believers to arise and walk in their rightful heritage, these shepherds are more often than not opposed by the debilitating and demonic mental plight of the sheep to whom they have been assigned.

Despite the fact that, as Scripture records, "even prophets and righteous men of old have desired to see what you see, and hear what you hear," the mindset of most believers today is one of callousness, irreverence, complacency, apathy and general ignorance of the essence of their "reason for being."

In short, though believers are matriculating through hundreds of "spiritual" conferences touching every conceivable theme, and although there is now unlimited access to Bible translations and computerized commentary assistance, the great majority of modern believers are so out of sync with the prerequisite submission to "apostolic authority" in their lives, that despite the overabundance of "Word," there is a corresponding inability to comprehend what is being spoken. They are, in essence, robbed of the good seed from which they are made fruitful!

Whether we like it or not, *the mind matters.* The proper orientation of the mind—which is the chief battleground for satan's schemes—is essential if we are to make a transformational difference in our lives, both individually and corporately, naturally and spiritually.

This treatise by my friend and brother, Dr. Jerry Kelly, deftly and articulately addresses this important prerequisite with apostolic boldness and a prophetic insight of uncommon dimensions. His message is a challenge to all forward-thinking believers, young and old alike.

As you read, it is my prayer that you will do so with an open mind and a teachable spirit. Yours is a destiny of greatness and power. You are called to walk in dominion and authority. However, the distance between where you are and where you need to be could be the current status of your mind!

Your dream is but a glimpse of a future reality prescribed in eternity and scheduled to manifest in time. It is a hint of God's untapped provision and of your untapped potential. It is a signal that God is ready to move you closer to your prophetic destiny.

The question is, are you ready to say yes? The journey will not necessarily be an easy one. But, with the insight of this book in tow, the journey will nevertheless be an understandable one. Destiny, now more than ever, is a matter of the choices you make. Accordingly, now more than ever we must accept Dr. Kelly's inevitable and insightful conclusion that the mind really does matter!

Bishop Harold Calvin Ray
Redemptive Life Fellowship, West Palm Beach, Florida

PREFACE

The world says, "The mind is a terrible thing to waste!" But I say it's a terrible thing not to find your mind and know its importance. Because people have not developed their minds as much as they could in regard to the faith principles by which to live their lives, when pressure comes they find they have no built-in plan to function effectively and make balanced decisions. Therefore, in the confusion of illogical or irrational thinking, people turn to drugs, alcohol and other hallucinogenic drugs for mind stimulation, because they have no resistance to pressure.

The vigorous and robust society that we are living in today applies tremendous forces of demand on the nobility of our minds. It takes distinguished, illustrious or superior minds to cope with the external environment we are exposed to in this so-called sophisticated, compound and complex modern society of ours. It encourages witchcraft and delving into psychic phenomena, and allows satanic deception, propaganda and pollutions to be imposed on our minds.

The mind may be defined as the seat or subject of consciousness, the thinking and perceiving part of consciousness or intellect, the unity of the conscious and unconscious, or simply that which thinks, perceives, feels and wills. When this vital organ becomes filled with the things and cares of the world, it is not "sound." When it takes on the consistency of, and logical connection with, the concerns and preoccupations of the world, our minds become at enmity with God, and we lose the ability and desire to understand the things of God. When our minds are characterized by this "carnal" mode of operation, we are wrapped up in a particular mental and emotional paradox: we become "ceremoniously insane," going through the motions in life and faith but behaving according to the mind-set of the world's system, which is controlled by the princes and principalities of darkness. In other words, we have not found, or lost, our minds! (See Luke 12:16-21 and Matthew 19:16-28.)

Success in life is based on accurate decisions, which begin in our thought life. A thought is a silent word; a word is an exposed thought. Everything in life starts in the thought form; after it is said, it is no longer a thought, but has become a word. From our words, we form ideas, which are the concepts of our thoughts made real or brought into reality. Ideas make up our potentials and abilities. However, ideas can come and go, and change; it is the imagination that transforms our ideas into plans. When an idea develops into an imagination, it becomes a plan or blueprint in our minds; it is not written or drawn out, but is something we have in hand, at our disposal—a visual display of our thoughts and ideas. If based on a sound mind, our imaginations are what cause us to build up the kingdom; if based on an unsound mind, our imaginations must be cast down as something that sets itself up against the knowledge of God (see II Corinthians 10:4). Therefore, we must be careful how we form our thoughts, ideas, imaginations, and in short, our minds.

We are living in a time of validation of personal mind-sets and "situational ethics." Long-established ideologies and immutable principles based on eternal truths are currently evaporating in the burning desire of revolutionary changes. The value of life has decreased, and the quality of existence diminished, because this generation of believers has lost its sense of destiny, purpose and urgency due to a carnal mindset.

In Philippians 4:8, however, we are encouraged to think

on the things that are true, honest, just, pure, lovely, of good report, virtuous and praiseworthy. If we make the qualification of our thoughts and judge them by these criteria, we will discern what builds the kingdom of God. If our thoughts do not qualify for our mind, they do not qualify for our mouths; if our thoughts do not qualify for our meditation, they do not qualify for our conversation.

If God's provision is blessing our efforts, we know that we are "geographically accurate"—in the right place spiritually, morally, intellectually, mentally, and in every other way that matters. *Where* we are in the body, soul/mind and spirit is as important as *what* we are as people. If we are in the place we are meant to inhabit, our own "promised land," we can receive favor, for God will bring the right people into our lives to connect with us for our prosperity in every significant way.

INTRODUCTION

Beloved, I wish above all things that thou mayest prosper and be in health, even as thy soul prospereth (III John 2).

The mind is a wonderful, intricate creation with treasures in store for those who persevere in its discipline. For example, you can go to seminars, purchase books, tapes and videos, as well as meditate on the Word of God night and day in obedience to the Holy Spirit, and as a result, become prosperous and "of good success." (See Joshua 1:8.)

By nature, your mind has been conditioned and programmed to fail before the new birth. III John says God wants you blessed, prosperous and successful.

The god of this world has blinded people's minds. There must be a reconditioning and reprogramming of your mind. (See Romans 12:1-2; Ephesians 4:23; and II Corinthians 4:4.)

The subconscious part of your mind has things that are deep-seated. The subconscious works to reject or kick things away from you; it indicates the deeper or inner mind and works by deduction. While you are working to get something *into* your subconscious, it is working to kick it *out*.

Renewing your mind means getting you free from all negative ideas. Negative attitudes become habits by repetition. You need to become a "book-aholic" and a "tape-aholic," reading and listening to positive input in order to counter those habits.

You must come to the point in your mind where you have an "ease of thought" about any topic. It is called being sound-minded or open-minded, with a teachable spirit.

How to Recondition Your Mind

Believing is an act of your will: you *will* believe or you *will not* believe. When you start understanding faith, you will change. When you have your mindset changed, you set in motion the things to change your situational ethics and your circumstantial evidence that has so bombarded you.

Carnal means in or of the flesh, materialistic or worldly, not spiritual; having to do with or preoccupied with bodily or sexual pleasures. *Enmity* means a bitter attitude or feeling, hostility or antagonism. It denotes a strong, settled feeling of hatred, whether displayed, concealed, or latent. Hostility is usually active opposition.

The world's system is always opposite to God's system. It is so important that after you become born-again, you allow the Holy Spirit to redeem your soulish realm.

The Holy Spirit sets up a classroom in your heart so He can teach your mind things about God that you will not forget. If you listen to Him, study the Word so that it can be engrafted in you and communicate with God in prayer, the Holy Spirit will keep your mind sound. (See James 1:21.)

II Timothy 1:7 says, "For God has not given us a spirit of fear, but of power, and of love and of a sound mind." I Corinthians 2:16 says, "we have the mind of Christ." Philippians 2:5 says, "let this mind be in you which was also in Christ Jesus."

Those whose minds are not yet "redeemed" to conform to the image of Jesus are called "carnal-minded." (See Romans 1:28.) Remaining carnal-minded leads your mind to becoming reprobate, unprincipled or depraved. When your mind is *unprincipled,* it's characterized by a lack of moral principles; you have a mind that is unscrupulous. You are without first law, rules or truth. Your mind is without the principle things.

The soul or mind is saved from day to day. It is called

working out your soul's salvation. It's an experience of bringing the soul or mind in line with the spirit and knowledge of God's Word. It is a progressive process.

When you have your mind renewed, it will affect your whole being. The mind is not accustomed to the things of God, and when you become saved and attempt to change the pattern of your mindset, it will fight you. Your mind feels it's under attack, and it will come up with all kinds of good excuses not to change. (See Ephesians 4:23.)

The renewing of the mind causes problems. To understand the things of God, there must be a renewing of the mind. God will stretch your mind! Once your mind is stretched, you will change. You must understand that renewing the mind is not optional, but a necessity. We are a naturalminded people, but we profess to live a spiritual and naturalminded lifestyle, with the spiritual mindset in control. (See II Corinthians 10:4-6.)

Remember, the things of God do not make sense to the carnal mind. The Word of God will transform your mind and renew the spirit of your mind or the functioning of your mind. The weapons of our warfare are mental ones. Faith is a weapon of the mind. When we have sound minds, we can lay hold on eternal life.

Strongholds of negative, degrading and fearful thoughts can be brought into the captivity of Christ. The Word of God can arrest the mind. You see, reasoning is man's way to live; faith is God's way.

You need to understand that God does not despise man's mind; after all, He created it. Until a Christian's mind has been renewed to the ways of God, that person really cannot think clearly. You must have a foundation of truth and reality to truly reason rationally. You must start with truth, or all of your reasoning becomes false—based on lies.

The voice of the mind is *reasoning*; the voice of the body is *feeling*. The voice of the body and the voice of the mind are influenced by outside environmental and external teachings which are inspired by satan, the father of lies. You are educated by the environment in which you grow up.

Science has spent millions of dollars to develop the physical body, and millions more have been spent developing man's intellectual processes. Man's spirit must be educated and improved, so that man's mind can be truly educated and improved. We cannot understand spiritual things with our natural minds. Our minds must be changed and renewed by God's power for us to fully understand the Word of God.

In James 1:21-22, James told believers if they want to get their soul/mind saved, they must be doers of the Word, not only hearers. James said to "receive" with meekness the engrafted Word, which is able to save your souls. In Romans 12:1-2, Paul reiterates what James said. Paul said everyone needs to be "transformed" by the renewing of their mind. Both apostles were talking about renewing, restoring and saving the mind or soul.

The reason God wants our minds renewed to the things of the kingdom is so our earthly minds can be lifted up to heavenly benefits. (See Isaiah 55:8-9 and John 8:14,23.)

Read Luke 12:16-21. The value of a man's life is not in the material things he possesses. Earthly things have no heavenly values.

Crazy is defined as a physiological malfunction of the brain that causes one to misbehave or malfunction, which is not the subject of this book. Jesus was not talking about that when he talked about losing your soul (mind). Losing your mind is when you let your mind get into a place contrary to the Word of God and letting it get into a place it was not created to be. Your mind was created to function in conjunction with the Word of God. Once we let our mind get outside of where it was created to be, that's what we refer to as having "lost our mind."

A renewed mind is a mind that is back where God wants it to be, so that our minds can function properly.

How to Avoid Losing Your Mind

1. Do not place your self-worth on what you possess. Never see yourself in light of what you possess. Your self-worth is what you are, not what you have, because *who you are* is the only thing that's going to stand, while *what you have* is going to perish.

2. Do not covet the possessions of others: it will cause you to misbehave, or lose your mind. When you start coveting the possessions of others you will do dumb things; you will do crazy things; you will let your mind get outside where God created it to be. You will start taking advantage of your neighbor; you will start to cheat, steal, take unfair advantage, or begin to do things that are unnatural.

3. Do not see possession of things as the answer to happiness. *Things* will not make you happy. *Relationship* is where happiness comes from.

4. Have no anxiety for the things of this world. Don't get so anxious about the things of the world. Anxiety is the devil's weapon to kill you. Patience is God's weapon to get you everything you need. Patience will get things for you; anxiety will take it away from you.

5. Do not be carnal-minded. The carnal mind is enmity with God. It will lead to sin and death. To be spiritually minded is to think like God. To be carnal-minded is someone who has lost his or her mind. To be spiritually minded is to keep your mind in line with the Word of God.

6. Do not keep your mind on the system of this world or rely on it; this will keep you from losing your mind. The system of the world will always let you down. You will always miss the mark with the system of this world; it is designed to fail. It is also designed to make you depend on it so that you will always come back to it.

The system of this world is self-centered. The system of God is kingdom-centered. It's centered upon kingdom principles and precepts. Once you become a believer, you ought to come out of the world system and operate in the system of God. You see, the key to the kingdom that Jesus gave us is so that we can access our kingdom benefits. The problem with the kingdom system is that it is contrary and sometimes foolish to the natural mind, and the devil uses it to cause you to have anxiety attacks.

The Word of God is supernatural; it's over the natural world. God's Word will elevate the mind over matter, over the physical world in which the five senses function. Losing your mind is when you let your mind get you out of the will of God's Word.

Personal or social change is only possible with a spiritual revival. The Word plants a seed in the womb of the thoughts to bring birth to new thoughts and ideas; this lifts your mind to heavenly benefits.

The Word of God is our connection to the supernatural. Our mind must be renewed to think on the level of the supernatural. (See I Corinthians 1:28 and I Corinthians 2:5,9-10,14-16.) Our mind must rule over matter, the sense realm—not bound to this material, natural and physical world. Our spirits are in touch with and live in the supernatural because our spirits are recreated according to II Corinthians 5:17—born again of God's spirit, which feeds the renewing of the mind.

Our spirit life is superior to the physical, natural or material life. We must not let our five senses, which are in touch with this physical world, dominate our lives because that would be a lower level of living. Natural living is a lower life than supernatural or spiritual living.

Man is a triune being: he is spirit, soul (mind) and body. The spirit is the true man; the body is the third dominion of man, the house in which the spirit lives in the physical sphere. The spirit is the higher form of living enclosed in the physical world, while the spirit of man communicates with the spirit or supernatural world. The physical or material is the lowest level or form of living, The mental or psychic is the middle level of living. The spirit is the highest level of living. The more you have your mind depend on the spiritual part of your being for its direction, the more you have your mind functioning correctly and the greater strides you will make toward living a full, victorious Christian life.

As you face the many challenges along the way in the process of growth, especially in regard to the mind, you will be rewarded with treasures at each level of positive change.

Chapter One
The Power of Mind Renewal

In this age of communication, the world's way of thinking about and doing things can so easily influence us. But God has said not to be conformed to the world's ideology.

And be not conformed to this world: but be ye transformed by the renewing of your mind, that ye may prove what is that good, and acceptable, and perfect will of God (Romans 12:2).

"And be renewed in the spirit of your mind" (Ephesians 4:23). God wants our minds renewed and elevated so He can make us whole and give us the direction we need to walk in the Spirit to bring His positive influence to the world in which we live.

Lay aside the filthiness and superfluity and abundance of naughtiness, and receive with meekness the engrafted *word, which is able to save your souls* [or to renew your mind] (James 1:21, emphasis added).

The word "engrafted" in Greek is *infortuitous*, which means "inborn" or "innate." When the word of truth is engrafted in our minds, it renews our way of thinking. It brings enlightenment and properly aligns us with the thoughts and ways of God for our fulfillment in purpose and destiny.

In John 14:2, Jesus said, *"I go to prepare a place for*

you." In verse 3 Jesus said, *". . . that where I am, there ye may be also."* You work with your minds. Many of us are accustomed to working with our hands. We have jobs in which we must routinely accomplish certain tasks by certain dates. But God created you to work your mind. Your mind must "go away" from you to a place that has been prepared for you. Jesus said, *"I go away to prepare a place for you, so that where I go, you may be also."* What He said may be interpreted as saying that we need to let our minds arrive at the place He wants us to be in the Spirit. But if we examine our minds honestly, we can determine that we are not yet where our Lord preordained us to be.

Ephesians 2:6 says we have been raised up together and made to sit together in heavenly places with Christ Jesus. Peter tells us that God has given us all things that pertain to life. Paul told the Church that we have been blessed with all spiritual blessings in the heavenly places, but our minds do not dwell there. Our minds are not in spiritual places where all the spiritual blessings are. Our minds are not working in the arena where we experience the living truth that "all things have been given to us that pertain to life and godliness." Why? Because we have no vision of it, our minds do not dwell there even though Jesus has already prepared the place for us. The reason we do not receive the Body of Christ and are, in fact, unprepared for it is that our minds resist doing so out of human weakness. Our minds are presently tied up in situational ethics—that which is right is relative to each particular situation and person involved. What is right for one person in one situation might not appear to be right to another person in the same situation. Situational ethics do not apply absolute principles, only subjective assessments which are not formed by the conscience, or an informed and correct mind. Circumstantial evidence carries more weight with us than the promises and the provisions that God has already made for us.

Proverbs 29:18a says, *"Where there is no vision, no revelation, the people perish* [or cast off restraint]." God wants to give us a mystical experience of seeing the supernatural so that we will never lack but will live in abundance. When you are not at the place where you can see the supernatural, you are going to perish. If you cannot look into God's Word and see the supernatural, you are going to perish, because God has prepared for us in the realm of the supernatural the place we are supposed to live in by faith. The richness of the Spirit makes all other visions pale in comparison—nothing even comes close to the surpassing knowledge and wisdom of God.

Proverbs 29:18b says *"but he that keepeth the law, happy is he."* Where there is no conscientiousness, there can be no responsibility. If we are not conscientious to keep what has been prepared, stored up, provided and given to us—everything that makes us who we truly are as God has made us, what He said we could have and accomplish—then we have no responsibility about us. And that's why believers are walking irresponsibly: Where there is no conscientiousness in regard to keeping the law—the principles and precepts of God—there is no responsibility, nor the added assurance that we are entirely where God wants us. You can only enforce what you know. Principles that should be applied to your life are not applied because your mind has not yet been renewed—the mind can't call up or remember what it does not know. *Ignorance* of the things of God is not bliss. We can only walk in the truth that has penetrated our minds and hearts. Therefore we need to look at increasing our spiritual receptivity, so that we may be molded in just the right way to hear and see what God has for us to enrich our lives and those of the whole Body of Christ.

Vision implies something that is, or has been, seen through discernment or perception, an intelligent foresight or a mental image produced by the imagination. Most believers know nothing about the imagination. In Genesis 22:17, God had to release Abraham to tell him what He intended for his inheritance. God said to him, "Abraham, look at the stars: you can count them." He had to project a vision into Abraham's mind to get him to start losing his old way of thinking. Abraham had to be willing to open up his mind so that he could go to the prepared place. He had to see God's vastly superior vision. He needed to submit his own understanding in order to receive God's blessings.

Ephesians 1:3 says, *"Blessed be the God and Father of our Lord Jesus Christ, who hath blessed us with* all spiritual blessings . . ." (emphasis added). II Peter 1:3-8 says,

> *According to his divine power hath given unto us all things that pertain unto life and godliness, through the knowledge of him that hath called us to glory and virtue: whereby are given unto us exceeding great and precious promises: that by these ye might be partakers of the divine nature, having escaped the corruption that is in the world through lust. And beside this, giving all diligence, add to your faith virtue . . . knowledge . . . temperance . . . patience . . . godliness . . . brotherly kindness . . . charity. For if these things be in you, and abound, they make you that ye shall neither be barren nor unfruitful in the knowledge of our Lord Jesus Christ."*

God wants to raise us to a new awareness of life—the divine life we are meant to participate in, and draw strength from, as our spiritual inheritance:

> *That the God of our Lord Jesus Christ, the Father of glory, may give unto you the spirit of wisdom and revelation in the knowledge of him: the eyes of your*

understanding being enlightened; that ye may know what is the hope of his calling, and what the riches of the glory of his inheritance in the saints, and what is the exceeding greatness of his power to us-ward who believe, according to the working of his mighty power, which he wrought in Christ, when he raised him from the dead, and set him at his own right hand in the heavenly places, far above all principality, and power, and might, and dominion . . . and hath placed all things under his feet, and gave him to be the head over all things to the church, which is his body, the fulness of him that filleth all in all (Ephesians 1:17-23).

Your imagination must be activated before you can allow your mind to enjoy all that we hope for and imagine. How do you get a vision, so your mind can grasp it? You must work your mind and force your imagination to spur your faith in God's power to bring it about. That's why the mind and imagination have been given to us. With any visual input or data, such as television, reading or seeing your immediate environment, we take that input and experience it first by grasping it mentally, without our having moved an inch.

Sometimes we can sit at home and be at our favorite vacation spot. Where are we? We're in the Pacific islands or in a secluded mountainy forest. In reality, you are not there—you're still sitting in the living room. We have to let our minds enjoy the promises God has given us. We can lose ourselves in God's promises.

In Numbers 13, Israel's problem was that they could not see themselves in the promised land. That's the problem with the Church: we can't see ourselves blessed. Numbers 13:1-2 reads,

And the Lord spake unto Moses saying, send thou

*men, that they may search the land of Canaan, which
I give unto the children of Israel: of every tribe of
their fathers shall ye send a man, every one a ruler
among them."*

Notice that they had to go and see it. These men were the eyes for the whole nation. But the only problem was that 10 of them were not ready for it. The promised land was a prepared place. For about 430 years, God had other nations prepare the promised land for them, but they couldn't see themselves in it; they couldn't release their mind to go to that prepared place. In Numbers 13:25-31, the Word reads,

And they returned from searching of the land after 40 days. And they went and they came to Moses, and to Aaron, and to all of the congregation of the children of Israel, unto the wilderness of Paran, and Kadesh; and brought back word unto them . . . and showed them the fruit of the land. And they told him, and said, "We came unto the land whither thou sent us, and surely it floweth with milk and honey; and this is the fruit of it. Nevertheless the people be strong that dwell in the land, and the cities are walled, and very great: and moreover we saw the children of Anak there. The Amalekites dwell in the land of the south: and the Hittites, and the Jebusites, and the Amorites, dwelled in the mountains: and the Canaanites dwell by the sea, and by the coast of Jordan. And Caleb stilled the people before Moses, and said, Let us go up at once, and possess it; for we are well able to overcome it. But the men that went up with him said, We be not able to go up against the people; for they are stronger than we.

Everything that the people saw in the promised land, God had told them beforehand that it was there. But they only saw the imposing people, and their hearts were not equal to the task. How many Christians worry about people? The believers' greatest problem is people. But when we act in faith, people cannot ultimately interfere in God's plans for us: God says rather, "What is yours is yours."

So the Israelites approached the land, but their minds were not prepared. Before you go to the prepared place, your mind has to be prepared. Many people get to where God wants them to be, but their minds are not with them—that's why we can miss our destinations and go ahead of God.

"And they brought an evil report of the land" (Numbers 13:32). When you get to the place where you are supposed to be without the knowledge of God, you are not going to receive it favorably. You cannot give testimony to what God has done in you if you are not aware of what He has done. You are more likely to tell somebody of the evil that God has given you. Can you imagine me telling you, "Yeah, well, God healed me, but I'm not keeping it." We don't know how we ought to respond because our perception is too often negative, because it needs to be enlightened. The Israelites needed to have their minds renewed so they could see the promised land from God's perspective.

The land, though which we have gone to search it, is the land that eateth up the inhabitants thereof; and all the people that we saw in it are men of a great stature. And there we saw the giants . . . and we were in our own sight as grasshoppers, and so we were in their sight. And all the congregation lifted up their voice, and cried; and the people wept that night (Numbers 13:32-14:1).

We need a vision of Canaan, the promised land, and the covenant promises and blessings of God, which have already been prepared for us. The Israelites had a poor image of the land and a poor self-image. What is a self-image? It is comprised of all the attitudes, attributes, perceptions, beliefs, emotions and feelings that you have about yourself. Self-image includes everything you perceive and believe about yourself. What reflection do you see when you look into the mirror at yourself? What do you see? Do you exclaim, "What a wretch!" Or, do you see yourself, "Um—my—would you look at that? I am fearfully and wonderfully made! Oh, thank God!" More often, you might return to criticize yourself, "How could God make such a drastic mistake?" What is your attitude about yourself? What are your motives, desires, ideas and visions? Are you ambitious one day, and the next day you are not? Are you thinking "Success" one day and the next day "Failure?" How do you see yourself? What do you believe about yourself with respect to success and productivity? What do you feel? How is your self-image enabling you to accomplish your goals and plans?

The reason self-image is so valuable and important is because out of self-image comes self-esteem, self-realization, self-value, and self-worth, which bring competence, confidence and motivation. Israel had a grasshopper-image, which bred negative thoughts and failure. But truth is based on purpose and destiny—not facts. When God told Jonah to go to Nineveh, truth was speaking. Jonah refused to go to Nineveh out of fear, and he jumped on a ship going to Tarshish (Jonah 1:3). He was thrown overboard and swallowed by a large fish. Jonah was supposed to drown to death, not only in the water, but also in the mouth of the fish. Water came in with him; he was supposed to drown.

Truth said, "Go to Nineveh." No fish could eat him up,

and no water was going to drown him, because truth said, "Go to Nineveh." So, God's truth changes or overcomes the facts of pressing situations. If we are stuck in a situation where circumstances do not promote us to be successful, we must remember God's truth. He says we can do all things because He has put faith in us. We have to stand on God's Word and go with it—not in our own strength—but taking strength from the fact that God has spoken. There's enough strength in what God has said for us to take on the world, to make waves out of still waters, to part the water of the Jordan river, to go where our promises are held. But many of us are wandering around naturally perceiving situations, which works against us. But truth changes situations and circumstances.

God's Word is truth. The reality of facts causes us to lose confidence. We wrestle with facts instead of accepting the truth of what God's Word is saying in a situation. When a lump appears on your hand, you have a growth. It is factual; you see it. But the truth says, *"With His stripes, we are healed"* (Isaiah 53:5). God says that He will supply all of our needs according to His riches and glory by Christ Jesus (Philippians 4:19). He didn't promise you that your job was going to do it—He said He was going to do it. Sure, the giants were in the land, and the people quaked in fear, but God said, "Go over and possess it." God's power will completely renew your self-image. You can be short and stand tall as a giant. You can have a lack of funds and still talk and walk like a rich man, if you operate in truth and pray to God. Loyalty means to change your mind and to obey the commands of God's Word, regardless of the factual situation and circumstances. Just be loyal to God's Word.

Sure, there are giants over there in the place we need to go. But evidently they are not going to bother us, and we will win. God said, "Go possess the land." "Giants, God told me to come and possess this land. So, since this is His word, either you get out of the way or die." Now, the believers see the giants and say, "I'm out of here!" The word of God should become a personal word to you, and you should eagerly obey it. This trust should defy our senses so we can instantly rely on the strength of God's Word. It is important because we need to live by the season of the Lord. If we don't follow God in the seasons, we've missed a season. Why? Because when God has something for you, He will let you know *when* He wants you to have it and *why* He wants you to have it, and He's the one that will make sure you get it. Go on the strength of God's Word. Israel had God's word, "Go over to Jordan." But here are 10 of them saying, "We're not able to possess the land; there are giants in the land." Thank God for Joshua and Caleb. Every Joshua needs a Caleb, and every Caleb needs a Joshua for company. There are people that God has ordained for our lives; we want to make sure that we stay with them. Otherwise, there will be people who will take us under, instead of helping us go over. Anytime people discourage you, God didn't send them. Two kinds of people come into our lives: ones that God sends and ones that the devil sends. When the devil wants to depress us, he puts people in our life. When God wants to make an impression on us, He puts people in our lives.

When has our visitation come? When Joshua went over, they met the captain of the host of the army of God. When is the timing coming from God? All Israel had to do was go over there when Moses was living. The same angel of the Lord that met Joshua when he went over there would have met Moses, if he had gone. But they never saw the angel of the Lord because there is a certain place they should have been before God would send them help from heaven. When we take that step, we are going to meet the angel of the Lord. Why? Because we called on the strength of the Lord. All we must do is step over Jordan, and the angel of the Lord will meet us there.

Things will change immediately for you in the spirit realm. God is going to send angels to fight our battles for us.

When we have an unhealthy self-image, the grasshopper complex creates multiple problems in our lives. How we see ourselves determines whether or not we will become a success or a failure, a victim or a victor. We need resourceful attitudes: these will help determine success or failure, victory or defeat. What we envision about ourselves is what we will become. See yourself as a failure when failure presents itself, and you will receive it and accept it because that is all you will see when you look within yourself.

Proverbs 23:7 says, *"As a man thinks of himself, so is he."* If you can't think of yourself as a "somebody," then think about Jesus. When you see yourself as a "nobody," then when opportunity presents itself for you to act like somebody or to become somebody, you will not accept it.

A few days ago a man said to me, "Nobody will give me a chance or opportunity. I can't do that. I just don't think I can do it, pastor." Well, who do you think can do it? "I don't know." Well, if not you then who? "I don't know; I just don't believe anybody around here can do it." Why do we start sizing other people up when the trouble begins as we decline to take responsibility and act. You will never stay down or defeated as long as you have a victorious relationship with Christ. If your relationship is with Christ, and my Bible says the Guy is a winner; so, I'm not identifying myself with anyone else but Christ. And that's who I'm looking at as the inspiration and measure of my success. When I get up in the morning and it just doesn't feel like Jerry can make it, I start looking at Jesus.

Our situation or circumstances should never determine our destiny. Just because we don't have any money now, we must not say we are going to be broke the rest of our lives. Don't say that you can't afford it just because you don't have the money right now. Say, "All things are possible," and believe it. Whether or not I have the money right now has nothing to do with it. If it's what God wants, I rely on the strength of God's Word. Destiny is not a chance, it's a choice. You don't need another chance; you need to make the choice that you are going to do it.

"No one will give me a job." You don't need a job; just get out there and use your hands. Go buy an old lawnmower for $12, and fill the gas tank for 79 cents. Start cutting grass. When you get enough money, buy a new truck, or buy an old used truck, even an old raggedy truck. Get that going, get the lawnmower going, and cut grass. Then you can buy a new truck and a riding lawnmower, then you buy another truck. Now you have a business, and you get other people cutting grass, and you oversee your business and employees. Start where you are successfully. You will always rise above the level of your circumstances when you have a victor's or winner's mentality. People who have low or poor self-esteem must cast from their minds the labels others have given them and their own negative, argumentative personalities. When we have a poor self-image or low self-esteem, we increase the level of impossibilities.

It is the *attitude* of our minds, not the *aptitude*, that determines the *altitude*. Our altitude determines how high we go. Our aptitudes indicates how smart we are. Our attitude is how we feel about ourselves; it's our self-image. If we have the right attitude of mind, we will go higher and higher and be successful. Fear of failure will take over when our minds are not sound or stable in God's Word, or in truth. We have a grasshopper complex when we are not faith-controlled; we are *fear*-controlled.

When we have a people-complex, we care too much about what other people think or what they are saying about us. Stop caring so much about what they think. When we have a grasshopper complex, we are self-conscious, people-conscious, and we feel rejection. What good can we do if we are not good enough to put ourselves into a position to bless someone?

The Bible says, *"Love thy neighbor as thyself"* (Luke 10:27). If you don't love yourself, you can't love your neighbor. "Do unto others as you would have them do unto you." I don't want anyone mistreating me. If anybody is going to bless me, I want them to bless me; if they are going to help me, I want them to help me. But, how are we going to get help from people who need help themselves? Brother, could you give me a ride to work? Hey, I'm trying to get downtown myself. Let's go over here and try. Now, you know no one will give both of you a ride.

We have got to get delivered from what other people think. Some of us will not go to college because we're afraid people might think we want to be somebody. You know what they say, "Well, my friends aren't going." Do you want to be left out like they are? Instead of being all hung up with, and held back by people, we had better get ourselves delivered from other people's unhealthy influence. That is what God told the apostle Paul:

> *But rise, and stand upon thy feet: for I have appeared to thee for this purpose, to make thee a minister and a witness. . . . Delivering thee from the people, and from the Gentiles, unto whom I now send thee* (Acts 26:16-17).

Some of us may have always suffered with an inferiority complex, feeling as if there was always somebody better than us. They probably weren't, but they put on a good front. When our mindset is that of self-hatred, self-rejection, and self-criticism, we believe everyone feels the same way about us. An unhealthy self-image brings unhealthy emotions; it stifles emotion, quenches motivation and reinforces hopelessness and weakness. Self-condemnation is the most destructive psychological attitude that a believer can have.

Revelations 12:11 tells how we can overcome all of this negativity, *"They overcame him by the blood of the lamb, by the word of their testimony; and they did not love their lives."* When God tells you to do something, get out there and do it. Lose yourself in God and watch Him bless you.

Revelations 19:10 says, *"For the testimony of Jesus is the spirit of prophesy."* Prophesy to your situation, to your own circumstance; rehearse what Jesus said about your situation. Speak the Word over it.

I John 5:4 says, *"Whoever is born of God overcomes the world and this is the victory that has overcome the world, even our faith."* People's labels, opinions, and failures of others do not matter; look to your faith. I John 5:5 says, *"Who is he that overcometh the world, but he that believeth that Jesus is the Son of God."* Jesus is our role model, who did first what we shall do (John 14:12). I John 5:14 says,

Now with the confidence that we have in him, that if we ask him, according to his will, he hears us. And if we know that he hears us whatever we ask, we know that we have the petitions that we have asked of him.

The healing has begun working on us. God shall perform it until the day of Jesus Christ. We can overcome poor self-image and low self-esteem by knowing deep-down that Jesus is the victor—knowing that in Him you can do all things because He has strengthened you. You can be what you want to be, and do what you want to do. I am blessed going in and I'm blessed going out. There is no light in my life without the Shepherd, and I should base my belief on Him. To every situation and every problem, I have a solution because I have the mind of Christ and the wisdom of God has come fully alive within me. Hear God's voice and cross over the Jordan.

I was born, bred, and raised in Hopewell, Virginia. The folks born in Hopewell continually worried about what other people thought. People sat around and talked about one another, but didn't do anything to help each other's situation. They would rather stay in the condition they were in than receive God's blessings. They need Jesus. We need to let God bless us as much as He wants to bless us. The spiritually needy have got to come and receive their healing. God in His mercy has brought us to the point that we must come to Him if we really want to live. The Church must cross over Jordan. The Bible says that Joshua and Caleb crossed over, and when they did, they ate their first products of the land, the manna. But after we have matured, we need to eat the fruit of the land. So many believers are still depending on the manna God sends, but are not fully depending on the One who sends it. We've got to start going there and making our own cake or wine, to start using what God has given us as raw material. We don't want to stay in the wilderness, living in fear of giants. If we see giants, that means that we have crossed over to Jordan. Giants don't ever show up until you start crossing and progressing. Just start praising God. God has brought us to triumph over the terrors that used to hold us back, keeping us from the incredible marvels God has for us.

Chapter Two
The Composites of a Sound Mind

II Timothy 1:7a reads: *"For God has not given us the spirit of fear . . ."* How many of us are walking in some form of fear? God doesn't want us to live in dread. What does He have in mind for us instead? *". . . but of power and of love and of a sound mind"* (II Timothy 1:7b). The spirit of power and of love is His gift to us, and it must be operated from a sound mind.

The mind is composed of intellect and will, and is the seat of emotions. It is the principal of intelligence, the spirit of consciousness regarded as an aspect of reality. It is the faculty of thinking, reasoning and applying knowledge. A sound mind constitutes a healthy mental state, something that heeds instruction and counsel in order to obey. The mind is something valuable to take care of.

In general, the intellect—the capacity of thinking, knowing, feeling, willing and making expression of emotion—is closely allied to judgment and reason. Intelligence applies to adaptive behavior, problem-solving, learning from experience and from deductive reasoning (extracting truth from a situation by viewing its components analytically). The mind has a rational faculty. Reasoning is a natural power of understanding. The mind also is constructed for reasonableness—the capacity for sound perception and judgment, a logical thought process that raises our comprehension, and the ability to evaluate and draw conclusions.

The Word of God should create in us a limbic system of high-powered truth. The limbic system in the brain consists of a group of interrelated structures that are concerned especially with our emotion and motivation. The Bible calls it "precept upon precept, and line upon line." We need the ability to express emotions and the will to accomplish what God has given us to do. For there must first be a willing mind in order to love and obey God's precepts (Psalms 119:5,40,45,56).

One cannot have such a willing mind without it being sound, for an unsound mind is a contrary mind. Many people walk around with a contrary attitude because they are without a sound mind; the tendency of their mind is to resist the things that lead to soundness of mind. Willingness is the key ingredient to a sound mind: we have to earnestly desire and pursue clarity, which comes from the God of order. He redeems our minds from the fog of confusion in this world. The measure of truth we attain is the degree to which we will be able to walk responsibly.

It is accepted according to that a man has, and not according to that a man has not.

Now, the Bible says in Proverbs 23:7 that *"as a man thinks, so is he."* His only bases of discernment are the knowledge he has gained of God's ways and whether his mind wills to accept and implement that truth into his daily decision-making process. That's why a sound mind is so important to be readily effective and responsive to the Word of God. Most of the time, our minds are not responding effectively because we have not been kind to ourselves by getting our mind renewed in the Word. God wants to show us that "there is more where that came from." Jesus encouraged Paul in this way, saying,

. . . I have appeared to thee for this purpose, to make thee a minister and a witness both of these things

which thou hast seen, and of those things in the which I will appear unto thee (Acts 26:16b).

The Church needs a sound mind, one that is becoming more and more aware of the revelation of God's ways of truth as we approach the eminent arrival of the 21st century. As we move further into what would seem to be the "last days," we ought to be filled with a new sense of urgency, which must be taken to another level of commitment. It is time to be urgent and diligent, to be prepared and ready for the Lord's coming.

We ought to "work while it is day, for when night comes, no man can work." An increased sense of urgency and appreciation of insight by the Church and its role and impact in the world must be worked into the infrastructure of our society. We are to be the salt of the earth, the light of the world, and the city that sits on the peak of the hill (Matthew 5:13-14).

But instead we are confused and double-minded because we don't know who we are and what we possess, and what our mission is as the Church of the living God. People are looking for a paycheck out of the Church. People are looking for a favor, stealing a relationship with God. It is because we don't know who we are called to be and what we are meant to do. We are playing games in God's house, and that's why the community is so dilapidated and so deteriorated. Because we, as a people that profess to be the children of God, do not allow the Holy Ghost to lead, guide and instruct us so that we can cause the community to be resurrected as the Word of God is preached to them.

Nehemiah 5:5 says, *"Yet now, our flesh is as the flesh of our brethren, our children as their children."* In other words, we are supposed to be living on a higher plane of life and in such a manner that our lives attract others to imitate our example. Our lives should be free of debt and full of abundance so that we can be a blessing, so that others have a desire to have what we have.

"And lo, we bring into bondage our sons and our daughters." We bring children—offspring—into this world. We bring them into this life and enslave them, put them into bondage automatically because they inherit our debt, or they inherit our pattern of getting in debt. They inherit our tradition of indebtedness because we are not free. *"And some of our daughters are brought unto bondage already."* Some of our daughters are brought into bondage already. Why? Because they duplicate themselves from our lives. That's why a mother that's on welfare has a daughter who is on welfare. . . and her daughter . . . and so on.

When you allow a child to come into this life and you have to lay the dependency of that child on the government, that child will grow up depending on the government. Some of our daughters are already in bondage because they have to automatically go right to the government for support. Some of our sons are also receiving governmental assistance because of our indebtedness, and our place and our stand in society. Now some are even accepting their children having children out of wedlock, giving them in their shame baby showers. When your nine-year-old daughter is giving a baby shower for your 17-year-old daughter who is having a baby out of wedlock, that is going to encourage the nine-year-old to do the same thing.

We are not giving our children enough firepower of faith principles to impact their lives for the better, and so we raise a generation to live in the same condition we are in. We must develop and enhance our internal resources so that we can give our kids the ability to overcome and triumph.

We don't need condemnation, but we do need to get free so we can walk in wisdom. We only reap what we sow. We want to sow good seeds in our children so that others will be blessed. We don't want our kids to pick up bad habits from us or others, and we don't want them to spread errors to others.

We don't want too much time to pass so that *"Neither is it in our power to redeem them."* We need to get out of that rut, whatever it may be, that holds us back from victory. We want to be good men and women who leave an inheritance for our children and our children's children.

Take your life into your own hands, and live righteously. A spirit of poverty affects our mind, and causes instability and impoverishment, and deprives us of the capacity for mind renewal. We've heard of mental blockage. Poverty puts a mental blockage on you. John 10:10 says that *"The thief cometh . . . to destroy."*

Destruction starts in the mind, as does failure and defeat. In Genesis 3:1-5, we find the woman influenced by Satan through the "eyegate," the "eargate," and the mind's pride. Why was the eyegate so important? Because it has to do with perception. The serpent told Eve, "You could be as God." Why? That was to arouse her pride. "You can know good and evil." He wanted to mess with her mind—her intellect and her emotion—for this critical, receptive area is where strongholds begin.

For the weapons of our warfare are not carnal, but mighty in God for pulling down of strongholds; casting down arguments and every high thing that exalts itself against the knowledge of God, bringing into captivity, every thought to the obedience of Christ (II Corinthians 10:4-5).

Strongholds result in destructive thinking. The reason people are so destructive in their thinking is because it is induced upon them through strongholds. When the enemy succeeds in constructing strongholds in people's minds, they become oppressed. Until they learn the truth of the Word of God, they will never be able to cast down those arguments in their minds against God and His Word. In Ecclesiastes 8:9, the Word says,

All this have I seen, and applied my heart unto every work that is done under the sun. There is a time wherein one man ruleth over another to his own hurt.

Do you understand that you can rule over a person so long until you hurt your own self? You can oppress another person only so long until you eventually wind up hurting yourself. That's why you find a lot of old people now with their minds messed up. They've been oppressed for 60 or 70 years, and oppression has destroyed their minds. Pride can make you not see the need for change, and you can even sit in church, not listen to and heed the Word, and your mind begins to go bad right there.

What you receive from God and apply to your life hinges upon your mind's reception of that revelation. The type of thoughts you think, reflect what you act upon from God. If you do not receive His word for you, you will actually miss out on God's blessings, according to James 4:3,

Ye ask, and receive not because ye ask amiss, that ye may consume it upon your lusts.

Acting only according to your thoughts, you tend to look for satisfaction or fulfillment in the wrong places, and God won't take any part in it.

God wants His power to be at work in our lives so that we can be all that we were meant to be—which is beyond our comprehension at present. Ephesians 3:20 says that God is

> *. . . able to do exceeding abundantly above all that we ask or think, according to the power that worketh in us.*

What is the power that works within us? It's in the Holy Ghost. That's why having a sound mind is so important: our actions must be directed by a sound mind, and not based on a depraved mindset. In Acts 26:18, God was sending the apostle Paul for this very reason,

> *To open their eyes, and to turn them from darkness to light, and from the power of Satan unto God, that they might receive the forgiveness of sins, and inheritance among them which are sanctified by faith that is in me.*

What inheritances are we called to receive? God, through His divine power, has given us all things that pertain to life. God has given us knowledge of Him so that we would have a sound mind and be able to keep the things that pertain to Him. A mind with the knowledge of God, responsive to Him, is blessed with clarity and peace, and functions effectively even under fire.

Colossians 1:12 says that God has qualified us to be *"partakers of the inheritance of the saints."* We are to be given the strength of wisdom and character to stand firm against all opposition and take our places in spiritual authority. God has qualified us to inherit every promise, every provision of the Gospel for believers who are delivered from the powers of Satan and delivered unto the kingdom of heaven.

His renewal of our minds transfers us to the kingdom so that we can receive the kingdom's benefits. Saints who know and are true to the Word of God are hearers who have received and been engrafted into His system, or have been impregnated with the Word to save their soul and have renewed and elevated their mind by the power of the Holy Spirit.

But there is a matter to be dealt with before we are set free: "matters" or worldly concerns are affecting your mind so that you think of nothing else (Mark 4:19). Because all you are thinking about are the matters of life. And when these matters are uppermost in your mind, it is impossible for your mind to be above your circumstances. We need our minds to be over matter, but not in the way that followers of Christian Science do.

When all you've got your mind on are the matters of life, there is no time to be a blessing to anyone else or to pray, because all of your thinking is consumed with the matters of life, and therefore your mind is not sound. You are not praying for your pastor; you're worried about bills. You sit in church, but can't hear the Gospel because you are worrying about where your husband is, that your son didn't come in, and your daughter didn't call. Matters are bogging down your mind. Leave them outside, and you come into church. You cannot allow what people say and do to keep you from serving God.

Therefore I say unto you, take no thought for your life, what ye shall eat, or what you shall drink; nor yet for your body, what ye shall put on. Is not life more than meat, and the body more than raiment? . . . Which of you by taking thought can add one cubit to your stature? . . . But seek ye first the kingdom of God, and his righteousness; and all these things shall be added unto you (Matthew 6:25,27,33).

Trust in God, and your mind will be over matters. You will have a sound mind. God will give you what you need and will see you through every difficulty. If we want to be His servants and witnesses, we simply need to place ourselves in His care and seek to do His will alone, and for us He *will* provide.

Chapter Three
The Law of the Mind

For I delight in the law of God after the inward man; But I see another law in my members, warring against the law of my mind, and bringing me into captivity to the law of sin which is in my members [my body and my soul] (Romans 7:22-23).

Looking at the word *law*, we find that it represents a systematic style of structure and a governor by which things must function. There are three laws that produce effects over natural forces and are at work on the earth: the law of God, the law of sin, and the law of the mind. God has a systematic way in which He works, by principles and precepts (see Isaiah 28:10,13). Sin works in a system, by lust, destruction and then death (see Galatians 3:13). The mind also works systematically, through the five senses, emotions, and thoughts. The battles of life are won or lost on the battleground of the mind.

Man is a triune being: he has a spirit, lives in a body and he possesses a soul or a mind. The soul or mind has four components: the will, the imagination, the emotions and the intellect. How you develop your mind spiritually, mentally, economically, socially and politically will have much to do with how you'll live your life—it can be healthy or diseased, prosperous or impoverished. Success and prosperity first originate in the mind, as well as failure and defeat. Most people who are defeated think it in their mind before it actually projects itself into their lives. That's why the Holy Spirit is inspiring you to realize that the mind matters. Yes, we need our spirits to be whole, and we desire our bodies to be healed, but don't forget that the mind matters.

People are walking around and their minds are gone; they have gone mad. We have failed in the area of mind regulation. People run wild in their imagination because they can't regulate it. The mind matters, for success and prosperity first originate in the mind; you must develop a successful mind. The only thing you were "born with" is a bottle in your mouth, but even for that you have to bite, kick, scratch and cry.

Christians have to be developed into maturity in this life. We are developed as we see the light. Many Christians are still "baby Christians" 20 years after they started following Christ; they have not made the progress they could have because their minds have never been regulated and renewed. The truth of the Gospel has to be applied. We have to expand a dormant and hypothetical mindset, to overcome the mentality that has been influenced upon us through our environment and society at large. You are influenced by your environment, whether or not you are aware of it or like it, for better or for worse.

This world and everything in it is temporary, subject to change, and it can change through biblical principles and precepts actively applied in your life. The mind's four composites of will, imagination, emotions and intellect determine whether or not you will experience the effectiveness of spiritual growth and God's knowledge of the truth. But there is always room for improvement.

For my thoughts are not your thoughts, nor are your ways my ways, says the Lord. For as the heavens are higher than the earth, so are my ways higher than your ways (Isaiah 55:8).

We could say that the degree of success we attain is determined by the extent we accept God's way of thinking. Now when we accept God's way of thinking, we have to let it take the place of our own. The old ways of thinking must be turned aside for something greater and more powerful. No man can serve two masters (Matthew 6:24), so why not place ourselves in the care of the One who is able to save us?

But even after we have entrusted ourselves to the Master, our mind must still be converted. It still may hold onto negative self-perceptions of the past. Proverbs 23:7 says, *"As a man thinketh in his heart, so is he."* You've got to watch how you think about yourself. So when you think evil about yourself, you've got to say about yourself what God says about you: He says you are blessed going in and going out. He tells you He'll supply all of your needs. Don't talk down about your situation or magnify your difficulties; focus on your position in Christ. Discuss the promises and covenant blessings He has given you and practice speaking "faith words" such as *"I can do all things through Christ which strengtheneth me"* (Philippians 4:13). Do not look at things the way they are—look at them the way they are going to be, for that is how God sees things.

If you look at how others are being blessed, you might get jealous. Work on persevering in faith and personal growth and thank God for what He *has* given you. No more will we be a reproach, if we build up our own walls (Nehemiah 2:17). If we say with Nehemiah that the hand of the Lord, which is great and mighty, is upon us, we will rise up and build and strengthen our hands for every good work (Nehemiah 2:18). That's the way you should always walk around in life. God is going to perfect that which produces the greatest effect upon us.

So built we the wall; and all the wall was joined

together . . . for the people had a mind to work (Nehemiah 4:6).

With a willing mind, much can be accomplished. In Nehemiah, the people had a mind for what they wanted to do, a mind to creatively and conscientiously rise above what they were already accustomed to doing. When you acquire wisdom, it calls out for change. You don't want to stay comfortable in what you are doing if it's not working. We need to get out of our "comfort zone" so we can get into a new level of life, get blessed, and be able to be a blessing.

Proverbs 24:3 says, *"Through wisdom a house is built, and by understanding it is established."* We have to understand what we know, and make it applicable. Wisdom builds a house, be it individually (body, mind, and spirit) or corporately: the Body of Christ and the house of God.

Before anything happens, we must prepare ourselves mentally by sitting down and encouraging ourselves with positive self-talk. Say to yourself, "Self, you are going to rise up and build. You are going to lay blocks for a foundation so you can get this skyscraper in my life built so that I won't deviate or toss and turn with every wind and doctrine; I want to build it on a solid rock. I want to place every block on a solid rock. I'm going to plumb the line so I can walk a straight line of holiness. I'm going to repair the breach in Christ. I'm going to return back to the old landmark. I'm going to build this wall so that I can walk down it, up it, across it and all around it and get blessed.

If you are not prepared mentally for a task, it will take a lot of energy out of you, and you still might be defeated. Whatever you're going to do, prepare yourself for it. You have to be prepared mentally. If you want to go to college, first prepare yourself mentally to go to college. You must accept all of the challenges. You must sit down and count the cost. You have to get motivated and go.

Most people are not likely to motivate you, especially if they haven't strived and achieved in that area themselves. They are prone to failure and are not going to encourage you to be successful. People tend to be jealous but will not do what it takes to get where you are. Therefore you have to build and encourage yourself. Begin by saying what you can do because God says you can do it. Along with that, be appreciative of what you've already done with His grace. I am from God, who is my source, therefore I am to have the same success that God has. Since God is successful, I am going to be successful. He's not a failure, so I'm not a failure. Why? Because God says I can do all things through Christ.

Reprogram the law and the pressure of your mind. Many make decisions in their life based on their comfort zone—the factual data with which they are comfortable. People don't want to change or be stretched, but it is impossible to get wisdom and *not* change. Wisdom will overpower ignorance.

God has given us promises, and made them plain through His teachings, but we don't want to change because we're comfortable just the way things are. We tend not to desire wisdom to make it applicable, because it is going to call for change. We know the blessings are there and they are ours, but for some reason we allow our human reasoning to reject them and our thought patterns to remain contrary to the ways of God, His Word, and what He has said about us.

Christians have so much trouble when stressful situations arise. The more they learn, the more they are responsible for what they know, and have to put it into practice. At times it is much easier to behave in our former ways of dealing with life. But staying comfortable can get us into predicaments, for it is easier to stay in sin than it is to get out. As a result, we descend deeper into confusion, and it doesn't get better for us.

In Numbers 14:1-4, the people questioned whether they had it better in Egypt and wanted to return. Ten of the 12 elders were talking negatively. They did not keep that evil report from passing their lips. They saw themselves as grasshoppers compared to the inhabitants of the land. But the only real difference between them was that the residents took advantage of their situation and made choices that caused them to succeed. The only thing that is preventing us are the choices we are making; time and opportunity for growth and progress belong to us all.

In Exodus 13:17-18, the people went through the wilderness instead of the land of the Philistines, even though the desert was not the most direct route. People do not like confrontation: they do not handle it well, and more likely they will respond to it by returning to former ways. But in the days of John the Baptist, the kingdom of heaven suffers violence, and the violent take it by force. But in order for us to gain what is really valuable in life, we must go against the grain. We can't look at circumstances and existing conditions. We have to get in there and take it. If God promised it, we must take it. First bind up the strong man, and then pillage his house (Matthew 12:29).

God wouldn't let the Israelites go the direct route because they were afraid of confrontation, so He chose a circuitous one that would get them there when they were ready—even if it meant allowing them to wander in the desert for 40 years. Much time could have been spent enjoying the abundant blessings of their inheritance, but they had to first get all the "Egypt" out of them—the negative attitudes and self-images they had acquired that needed to be straightened and healed.

The choice is ours to make whether we are to press on, giving God permission to go as swiftly as possible in what He wants to teach us and how He wants to perfect us. First we have to prepare our minds to receive His promises. But we as

Christians are afraid of confrontation when it comes to the Kingdom. We ourselves are sleeping giants needing a wake-up call. The battles of the righteous are won with the boldness of a lion. Tell the enemy to get out of your way. Bold as a lion, take what you want and devour.

We cannot afford to be chicken-hearted or cowardly. The Israelites had the verification of the promised land: it was just as God described it. They had a decision to make, and they decided that they knew better than God. Their self-image as a people was dissimilar in nature to what God saw and knew about them. So you have to be careful how you see yourself and what you think about yourself. Remember what you possess, or you're going to be taken down, you'll compromise and wind up defeated every time at every turn.

Instead of "throwing in the towel," throw the towel away and say, "I'm in for the duration. I'm going to fight to the finish, because I know when the bell rings, I'll win." You must fight like Muhammad Ali: when you hit the ropes, you've got to come back with even greater intensity. *"Fight the good fight of faith"* (I Timothy 6:12). Do not behave like one that's already beaten before you go in. Zero in on your target: look at sin and knock it out of your way. You need to look at poverty and infirmities and knock them out of your way. Fight with all you've got. Stick to the fight when you're hardest hit: it is then that you must not quit.

Christians can give up too quickly if they make a decision contrary to true facts, because of their negative self-image. How you perceive yourself today is how you will be tomorrow and how you will affect others to perceive you and treat you.

But if you say that you have been created with all the talents needed to triumph over circumstances because of the purpose you have to fulfill, things will change in your favor. You need a purpose and God's inspiration to encourage you believe it is possible and attainable. When you start thinking like God, your ways change and you come to appreciate the increase in effectiveness and peace.

Matthew 6:31 says that we should "take no thought saying" anything other than what God has spoken for our wellbeing. Thoughts are incorporated into our thinking and our person when spoken. We must choose to accept what God has designed fitting and appropriate for us. He has all that we need, and if He doesn't have it, we don't need it. Constantly choose to change your thoughts and your environment so that they come closer and approximate what God has in mind for us. Choose the right environment so thoughts won't attack our minds and cause us to stray from the quickest route to our salvation.

Many people are incoherent in their thinking—a fact that can be recognized in their behavior and their mannerisms. They are not consistent in their behavior and their thought life because they have dysfunctional thought patterns.

Proverbs 21:5 says, *"The thoughts of the diligent tend only toward plentifulness."* Proverbs 10:4b says, *"The hand of the diligent maketh rich."* If we can manage our minds, we can control the quality of our lives; if we can control our thought life, we can regulate the quality of our lives.

Chapter Four
The Readiness of the Mind

These were more noble than those in Thessalonica, in that they received the word with all readiness of mind, and searched the scriptures daily, whether those things were so. Therefore many of them believed; also of honourable women which were Greeks, and of men, not a few (Acts 17:11-12).

God is looking for openness in our intellects and wills—a willingness to admit we do not yet know everything and the eagerness to find out what we still lack. The word *noble* means fair-minded, openminded, and having or showing high moral qualities or ideals. *Noble* can also mean more courteous, of a better deposition or education; having excellent qualities; superior; grand; stately; high hereditary rank; aristocratic. The quality of your life is an indication of the type of thoughts you think.

The word *readiness* indicates a ready quality or state of mind, that a person's life is a living expression of the usage of his or her mind. Once a truth is made known to us, it is aggressively acted upon. Grasshoppers are more likely to let grass grow under their feet; we want to run like cheetahs once we have spotted a herd of gazelles: 65 to 70 miles per hour—the fastest an animal can run on land. In II Corinthians 8:10-12, we read,

And herein I give my advice: for this is expedient for

you, who have begun before, not only to do, but also to be forward a year ago. Now therefore perform the doing of it; that as there was a readiness to will, so there may be a performance also out of that which ye have. For if there be first a willing mind, it is accepted according to what a man hath, and not according to what he hath not.

We need to continue to learn and progress with the same vigor and fervor with which we began. With a ready mind, there will also be a ready will. In order to have a ready will you have got to overcome the mentality that has been formed and shaped in you from your environment, and other external influences of negativity.

Success is adapting to God's way of thinking, which is positive. Never will anyone find anything negative about God's nature. All things are possible to Him—and because of Him—to you. Jesus came so that you may resurrect and elevate your minds. He said, "I'm from above, and you are from below." Get your mind elevated so that you will live a kingdom life, instead of a normal, natural life. God's way is a superior life, but it can only be lived in the realm of the spiritual revelation and perception.

Many people are successful, but their minds are not peaceful, for serenity comes with accepting God's will when it is not comfortable and agreeable to our senses.

In II Kings 5, Naaman was told by the prophet Elisha to go and wash in the Jordan river seven times in order to receive his healing. But Naaman went away upset, as a person will do when he does not have a willing or a ready mind. If he had readiness of mind, Naaman would have obeyed the word instantly. But he came with his own ideas of the way he should be healed. *It*'s divine providence and we can't call the shots—we'd make a mess of things. We need the healing,

God has the healing power, and so we humbly have to take it the way He sends it.

But Naaman's attitude was, "I am not going to dip in no muddy Jordan." The Jordan was a muddy river, and the rivers of Samaria ran with clean running water. He wanted to know, "Why can't I go and dip in one of these other clean rivers?" Why can't we just have a readiness of mind to obey God? We have to dip into the Jordan because the prophet of God says so. Many people miss their blessings because they refuse to have a readiness of mind. They need to have a renewal of the mind so as to hear it, believe it, study it and act on it.

Naaman brought along with him the equivalent of $77,000 in gold and silver. He had his hopes high at first; he was willing to make the prophet Elisha rich, but he became belligerent because he was told to do something other than what he thought should have been done. Because he lacked the readiness of mind, he resisted revelation and healing. All he had to do was be willing.

Do you understand the seriousness of leprosy? A few years ago, Pastor Jones and his wife, Pastor Linda, and my wife, Pastor Brenda, and I, went with others to Panama on three different occasions on crusades. While there, we saw true leprosy. One man's whole nose was gone. You could look back up into his head. We saw some with legs eaten off and holes in their knees. This is real; we saw the real Bible's truth over there. Leprosy is an awful disease that just eats away at a person. Do you understand the devastation that Naaman had to be in mentally? And here's an opportunity for him to get healed, just by bathing in some muddy water, and he didn't want to do it because of *pride*? That is what's wrong with churches: pride is depriving the people of all that God has provided. We have to get rid of pride and obey God.

Where were we when God made the stars, stretched out the valleys, pushed the mountains up, hung the moon and swung the sun in its orbit? Where were we? Listen, we better get in the muddy water! Many people make decisions in life based only on what they know, what they think and what they are comfortable with. But God uses the foolish things of the world to confound the wise (I Corinthians 1:27). He can raise "sons of Abraham" from the very stones (Matthew 3:9).

We need to learn to see in darkness, to just hear God and obey—not understanding it or seeing the reality of it—but because He said it. Unquestioning willingness and a militant quickness to obey are required to move in the way of the Lord. He will show us the wisdom behind His directions later, but first we must trust Him. We want to say, "Tell me what it is, and I'll think about it." But God asks us to accept His will, and then He'll tell us what it is. He knows how we think; the Son of Man knows what is in the hearts of men.

We want to rationalize everything and look into everything carefully before we do it. But we've got to accept God at His word. We fight for our own causes, but when God says to do something, we say we've got a problem with it. We doubt Him from whom all wisdom and blessings flow.

Truth is based on purpose and destiny—not facts. A lot of us try to live out of the realm of facts, and that's our problem. The current statistics say that 50% of all marriages break up. My Bible says that my marriage can last because God is in it. I don't care if the statistics go up to 99%, the only one left is going to be my marriage. If we want a change in our lives, peace, stability in our marriage, hope, the ability to reach destiny and fulfill a purpose, we better dip in the muddy water and give our minds and wills—our entire lives—to Jesus.

Loyalty means we change plans to meet the requests of the leader. Therefore, Naaman had to change plans. He had to get rid of his fantasy about the man of God waving his hands over him and getting an instant miracle. It would have been easier if the man of God had done it all, but God wanted Naaman to get to a level of obedience so that he could receive his healing and stay healed. All he had to do was have a readiness of mind. We must rid ourselves of reluctance to obey. God knows just what we need; we need to trust that He'll provide for us and lead us through everything that comes against us, especially when it comes to carrying the cross or carrying out the mission He has for us. The following story, entitled "The Cross Room," expresses the truth about our human nature—our tendency to want to avoid the burdens and responsibilities we have in favor of lesser evils.

The young man was at the end of his rope. Seeing no way out, he dropped to his knees in prayer. "Lord, I can't go on," he said. "I have too heavy a cross to bear."

The Lord replied, "My son, if you can't bear its weight, just place your cross inside this room. Then, open that other door and pick out any cross you wish."

The man was filled with relief. "Thank you, Lord," he sighed, and he did as he was told. Upon entering the other door, he saw many crosses, some so large the tops were not visible. Then, he spotted a tiny cross leaning against a far wall. "I'd like that one, Lord," he whispered.

And the Lord replied, "My son, that is the cross you just brought in."

We need to understand that *"the weapons of our warfare are not carnal"* (II Corinthians 10:4). Naaman had a carnal mindset. He wanted to fight the spirit of corruption which caused the leprosy by his own fantasy, according to his own thoughts. Sometimes because of who we think we are, our minds argue with God.

II Corinthians 4:18 says, *"We do not look at things which are seen, but at things which are not seen. For the things which are seen are temporal and the things which are not seen are eternal."* Naaman couldn't see the eternity or the power of God in that water; all he could see was mud. You have to be able to look through the mud and see God's provision.

Naaman went away offended. Offense is undigested revelation. He left, not even understanding that what he came for—came to pay for—was in the muddy water. A person's nature is revealed when he is under pressure. Naaman's nature was fully revealed. He was a proud man: he had all that money and needed healing, and left with pride.

When he finally obeyed God and did what God said, dipping in the river seven times, his skin was so nice it was just like somebody had just smacked him on the behind in the emergency room: it was like brand-new baby skin. When you obey God and come up out of that mud on the *seventh* time, you are going to be *perfect*. They didn't have mirrors in those days, so he said, "Servant, how do I look?" "You look like Billy Dee Williams!"

Naaman made a decision contrary to the Word because of the image or perception he had of the river. He allowed the outward appearance to affect his decision, instead of obeying the man of God. God spoke to him at that time. Decisions made today will always have future ramifications. You have to organize and arrange your thought life so that you can begin to get out of the situations and circumstances you are in. It is not left up to chance: it is a matter of choice. If you are not satisfied with the state that you are in, you need to know that it is only going to change when you begin to rearrange the thoughts of your mind. Obedience, work and accuracy are required to train yourself to formulate facts of truth and make right decisions that will give you the positive effect you desire.

If you can control your thought life, you can regulate the quality of your life. Life is *choice-driven;* it's really about *making choices.* You have some say in what you are going to experience in life through your attitude. You control your attitude by submitting inconsistent thoughts to the laws of a renewed mind. If your emotions are ungovernable, your life becomes disorderly and devoid of God's blessing. The Word is our source, not our environment or our investment in all of those things that we deem so important in life.

You can be a born-again believer and miss your inheritance. Your mind really matters, but it also must be baptized and renewed in the Word of God. The Spirit of God said that your thoughts and ways are no longer to be your own, because you now have the mind and heart of Christ. Forget your own thoughts and your own ways, and He will show you great and mighty things. The Lord says that if His people humble themselves, relinquish pride, and commit to His way of thinking and doing, then He will deliver them from their destruction and give them rest and peace, and meet their needs according to His richness and glory.

In Matthew 14:28, when Peter saw Jesus walking on the water, *"Lord, if it be thou, bid me to come unto thee on the water."* Peter had readiness of mind. The Bible said Peter stepped out of the boat and walked on the water.

The "doubting Thomas" said, "I won't believe it until I can see the nail print and thrust my hand in his side." Jesus appeared in the midst of the apostles and said, "Thomas, listen. Blessed are they that believe without seeing. But look at the nail print in my hand and the wound in my side." Be of a ready mind—a willing mind—because God has already provided everything He desires you to have. Peter told us in the Word that God has given us all things. Paul said that He has blessed us with all spiritual blessings in Christ Jesus.

The Church has got to make the mind matter. But we must allow it to speak to the matters and tell them to move out of our way. We need to have a clear conscience and a ready mind, handing our will over to God. Our bodies will become motivated like a diver on a springboard to His work. Our minds will be sharpened, honed, or sensitized to receive the blessings of the Spirit and operate with clarity and precision.

God told Paul to go and preach the Gospel to the Gentiles that they might have forgiveness of sin and receive "an inheritance among them which are sanctified" (Acts 20:32). Our inheritance lies right in our hands, right in front of us. It's one act of belief away. Reach out with the arms of faith and have a ready mind to believe the truth of the Word so you can be a witness to other people about the goodness of the Lord. The Lord said, "My people, I want you to come up a little bit higher. I have great and mighty things which you see not, but I'm ready to reveal them and put them in your heart, and put them in your mind for you to go forth and do great and mighty things. Your eyes have not seen it, but you've heard it. Move up higher; come up higher."

All of the silver and gold, and all the cattle on a thousand hills belongs to God. Blind people have no business being in the light. The Bible said worship the Lord above all things, that all men will prosper. It is predicated on your mind prospering, depending on how you believe, on how you will your mind. You've got to give yourself completely to God, fast and pray, and give until it hurts, being holy—separated and consecrated—for the willing purpose of God.

Chapter Five
The Nomadic Mindset

The people of Israel had enough of God's leading and thought they could do better on their own, returning to Egypt. They were restless and dissatisfied, and displayed what we will call the "nomadic mindset." The root word *nomad* indicates a person who roams about, a wanderer. A nomad is a member of a people who have no fixed residence but move from place to place, or is simply an individual who roams about aimlessly in life. The person with the nomadic mindset will always live in "no-man's-land"—an unclaimed or unowned piece of land better known as the wilderness. This land can be quite easily under dispute by two opposing parties.

A man's mind needs training for positive development. Israel, as a people, had been brainwashed for 430 years. They had been in captivity and under the oppression of a strong taskmaster; their minds had been controlled. They were in a state of dependency. The Bible says that when a person controls what you see, hear and understand, you become inferior to them and to anyone that you come in contact with. Not only did they feel inferior to the Egyptians, now they felt inferior to the people of the land that God told them they would possess. They became a people with a nomadic mindset, dwelling in no-man's-land. People that own and possess nothing have nowhere to go, so they always want to return back to bondage.

What we believe is a result of our thinking. If we think wrongly, we will believe wrongly and our ways will be in error. If our believing is wrong, the confession of our mouths or what we say will be wrong. Everything hinges on our thinking: our mind matters a great deal. Thoughts come and go, but our mind remains.

The people were going somewhere, but their thoughts and ways were not the Lord's (Isaiah 55:8). They wandered around in the desert for 40 years, not owning a thing—not getting to where God intended for them to go. They did not know that the wilderness was a place of preparation for them, and so for them it was only a no-man's-land. God doesn't waste any opportunities; we don't take them when He offers. Man thinks way too small, and his ways reflect that narrowness of perception. Our thinking must be in line with the Word of God, which has been given to us to straighten out our thinking. But too many of us, with our nomadic mindset, want to rationalize the Word to make it conform to our lifestyle. God's Word has ultimate authority on what's right and what's wrong. God created all things by His Word. You can only believe what you know; what you don't know, you can't believe. Proverbs 23:7 says that we are the product of our thoughts: what you have or do not have, what you like or do not like, is a direct reflection of your thoughts. So if you have a problem in life that you are unsure how to handle, check out your thought patterns.

Most believers are living below their privileges because they lack the knowledge of who they really are and *whose* they are. Proverbs 3:5-6 says,

Trust in the Lord with all thine heart; and lean not unto thine own understanding. In all thy ways acknowledge him, and he shall direct thy paths.

Believers trust in the Lord, but they fall short because they lean to their own understanding; they trust in their own intellect, feelings, and emotions. Many believers' minds are wandering because they do not know the truth of God's Word, which holds the key to their identity and destiny. They live in no-man's-land, not knowing who or what to believe. Israel listened to the ten fearful spies instead of the two spies who were operating in faith. Even in the promised land, they were without a land to call their own.

How many affiliate with God in the midst of our fellowshipping? Our thoughts are running wild, and our imaginations are not "kingdom domesticated," but are uncultivated in God's principles and precepts. If we would allow God to school us in the excellent science of the saints, what *wouldn't* He do for us and through us?

But many believers' emotions are ungovernable, resulting in their lives being disordered. The Body of Christ is out of control. Why? Because of the nomadic mindset. They are wandering from church to church.

James 1:8 says, *"A double-minded man is unstable in all his ways."* Most Christians love a pastor until a message comes their way for their correction. They love a church until they can't have their way. Many believers are living in total confoundedness. Their lives are not fruitful. They are bored, distressed and stressed out. Thank God for a remedy. Joshua went out there and said, "We are well able to possess the land. We can do it, and God told us to do it." But many Christians want to stay where they are comfortable. But when God moves, you better move; without His direction and provision in the cloud by day and fire by night, we are lost. We can't survive without Him because He's our source.

Israel wandered around for 40 years in the wilderness, and there they died. The only choices they felt were available to them were to either stay in the wilderness and die, or go back to Egypt and live in bondage. Because they couldn't get themselves free, beginning in their minds, the option of taking and possessing the land never came up. Their nomadic mindset could not lay hold of the land because they did not take advantage of the opportunity for preparation. If you fail to plan, you plan to fail. If believers put the same energy into faith as they use to wiggle out of responsibility, to respond with faithfulness and commitment, they would be receptive to God's plans and they would be blessed more quickly. It takes more energy to try to get out of things that are right than it does to take the same energy and use it to do right. Unsound minds miss out on the blessings that come with obedience to the directives of the Lord. He only wants the best for us, so why do we resist, preferring our own way—even though it gains us nothing in comparison? Our minds need to be born again of the Spirit.

Do not try to depend on your own understanding—you don't have enough of it. Trust the word of God. When you lean to your own understanding, your reasoning and your imagination develops powerful arguments against the logic of God. God's wisdom consists of authenticity and power. Your mind will naturally argue with it, "I don't see why God said we must do this. I don't see why God said we must do that. I don't see why I can't go here. I don't understand why I have to stop doing this." It doesn't make any difference if you understand it. God said you must, so you just do it.

But if you won't obey God, you won't obey your doctor, or your boss, or your pastor, or anyone, and you'll always have a problem with someone or something that is said or done. The doctor said you have high blood pressure and you should stop eating pork; you therefore choose to give up pork chops but start eating ham. You can't fool cholesterol; it is going to work against you all the same. So you are always trying to fool somebody, trying to get around what you need to do.

Your thoughts will denote your ways; if your ways do not please God, you cannot reap your inheritance among the saints. You become tired of aiming for perfection. God will let you go with them, but you won't *shine* with them.

We can't get around the truth and still be blessed. We can't fool God, but only fool ourselves in the process. We need grace to do what is right because it is good for us. Even more, we want to come to love to do what is right and good because God is goodness and truth Himself. Father's true worshippers worship Him in spirit and in truth (John 4:23-24). We have to love the truth and hunger and thirst to acquire it in order to get closer and closer to Jesus, our source of the true "good life."

In Proverbs 16:7, it is written, *"When a man's ways please the Lord, even his enemy will be at peace with him."* How many of us know that we—meaning our minds—are our own worst enemy? I thank God when he changed the enemy in my mind, so I could think clearly.

Many of us have "runaway minds." If people could see some of our thoughts, they would run from us. If we realized how we are thinking at times, we would run from ourselves. Half the time we don't know who we are in Christ, where we are in our relationship with Him, and that our own thoughts are holding us back from knowing Him better. Worst of all, we don't know where we're going, or who we are, and we are going nowhere quickly. Let's come to church to get more and more right with God, as truths are made known to us.

The only way we can have the mind of Christ is to study His Word, believe it in our hearts and ponder it so that it stays with us. Philippians 4:8 teaches us to think on whatsoever is true, honest, just, pure, lovely and of a good report. The 10 spies did none of that; they gave an evil report. Any time you say something that is contrary to what God says, it's an evil report. And you can ruin people's lives running your mouth when you don't know what you are talking about. They caused the whole generation to die in the wilderness because of their perception from a nomadic mindset.

Usually, there are two types of people: the ones who are going to help you overcome in life, and ones that are going to take you under. Very few will help you, because most people are selfish. They don't care if you overcome or go under. Usually, if you try to progress before they are ready to do so, they will attempt to hinder you. So, if your trust is in people, you cannot overcome, but will succumb instead. People do not want you to get what they do not have. They will try to snuff out the light of goodness in their midst because it convicts them that perhaps they are not going far enough in their walk with God.

Draw nigh to God, and he will draw nigh to you. Cleanse your hands, ye sinners, and purify your hearts, ye double minded (James 4:8).

In Acts 9:5, we are instructed not to *"kick against the pricks,"* resisting what we really want and need, as Paul did. Jesus had to show Paul that he was persecuting and fighting against God—his own source of life—and even himself. Jesus had to reveal to him his spiritual blindness, for "zeal without knowledge is foolishness."

The only way to get rid of doublemindedness is to get knowledge and understanding, which comes through grace and truth. Thoughts can come into your mind from two different sources. You have to know your true source. In other words, the thoughts that come into our minds do not always originate in our minds. The devil puts many thoughts into our minds from outside of ourselves. The other source comes from within, when God speaks to our spirits and our spirits reveal that truth to our minds.

This book of the law shall not depart out of thy mouth; but thou shalt meditate on it day and night, that thou mayest observe to do according to all that is written therein: for then thou shalt make thy way prosperous, and then thou shalt have good success (Joshua 1:8).

When you allow this word to get down into your spirit, it will come down to the point where it becomes transferable—so that it communicates from your spirit to your mind, so that your mind can grasp the revelation of it, and the illumination of your mind will explode within your life to help conform it to the image of Christ. Your ways will become just because your mind will be filled with the thoughts of Christ. God's Word is your source: stay in close fellowship with that source, through prayer, meditation and study. When your thinking is straightened out, and your believing and confessions are made right, then it will be much easier for you not to labor in your Christian walk, which will result in your having and reaping what you desire from the Lord. That is, you will have and receive the inheritance.

I am reminded of a prodigal son who left his father's land and wasted the inheritance that was coming to him from his father (see Luke 15). He spent all of his wealth, and he wound up in no-man's-land—in a pig pen. Too many believers are living in a pig pen. They are wallowing in the mud in a nomadic mindset. They don't know who they are and where they are, and don't know what to do. The prodigal son said, "What am I doing? Where am I going? I've got to wise up and go back to my father's house." When you repent of your sins, and you confess the name of Jesus, you will come to your senses. Imitate the nomadic man who got delivered of his affliction, was clothed and in his right mind and desired to follow Jesus (Luke 8:35).

Beware of the pig pen. When you are in the pig pen, you are eating pig slop. Let's get up and get in our sound mind, and get back in the church. The Father will place a ring on your finger and golden slippers on your feet. There will be a party for you—the party of rejoicing. All in the heavens will praise God.

Pigs will eat anything, and they'll eat anywhere, but their only problem is their nature. A pig's nature remains unchanged: after you clean them up and give them something good to eat, they want to go right back to the pig pen. But sheep will only follow and eat at the place to which the shepherd leads them. They will follow the leader and reside in beautiful countrysides. The Lord is their shepherd; there is nothing they shall want (lack). Beside verdant pastures he leads them for his name's sake (see Psalm 23). The shepherd stands by, continually watching over his flock, protecting them from predators.

But the pigs are left unattended. In Mark 5:1-20 the demons asked Jesus to be sent into the pigs, because the sheep, being submitted, would stay put. When pigs get hot, they always run to water to cool off. They ran in the wrong direction, blindly seeking relief, which is what the demons wanted, running from Jesus' presence. Instead of running down the slope, into the river, they should have run to the well up the hill.

Chapter Six
The Mind Matters I

In Genesis 1:26-31, God saw everything that He had made, and found everything to be good. God created the animals and brought them to man and told him to name them (Genesis 2:19). So when God created Adam, he was of a sound mind. Adam was so blessed with the attributes of God permeating his mindset that he was knowledgeable enough to look at the nature of everything that God had created, and name it. He had vast wisdom and a functioning, intelligent mind that was able to perceive the perception that God had about everything that he had created, and he was able to name them because he knew their nature.

But, as the Word says in John 10:10, *"The thief comes, but to steal, to kill, and to destroy."* In Genesis 3, satan came into the garden of Eden in the form of a serpent, to deceive Eve and to destroy God's man. He cast doubt upon what God had said; he knows the mind is the decisive battleground of our lives, and if he can conquer that, he can conquer your spirit and your body. He suggested to the woman to eat of the fruit God had prohibited, for it really wouldn't hurt her but help her. Here he is stimulating a thought—a negative thought or deception—in her mind. The mind was created to absorb, ascertain, and perceive knowledge. So he stimulated her mind with false knowledge.

He told her she would not die by disobeying God, but would become like Him, knowing everything, including the knowledge of good and evil. They already had God's perfect view of everything in the world. What the enemy offered was sin knowledge—a view of the world through jaded, distorted, cynical, warped vision. In place of God's complete panoramic view of the best of life, he offered a view of reality of their own making—how they wanted to see things—disguising the fact that they were losing a great deal and would forever have to struggle to get it back in part. He was messing with her mind, turning her focus from God to herself. As soon as she partook of the fruit, she would die spiritually, and satan knew it. But "misery loves company."

There are three ways to get to man: through the lust of the eyes, the lust of the flesh and the pride of life. These are the avenues by which he entered in to start the battle in Eve's mind. *"And when the woman saw that it was good for food,"* her curiosity was aroused and a visual perception overpowered her mind, which stimulated thoughts. So you have to be careful what stimulates your mind, because it will project a vision. Then Eve perceived that the fruit was good for food, *"And that it was pleasant to the eye"* (Genesis 3:6a). The lust of the eyes grabbed her senses. Next, she found the tree *"to be desired to make one wise."* Her mind was captivated. The pride of life enticed her, and not only did she eat, but she induced Adam to follow her example as well. Now, it's one thing for the serpent to deceive Eve, but then she turns around and deceives Adam (Genesis 3:6b). In verse seven, we read,*"And the eyes of them both were opened."* We readily spread our newfound "knowledge," which is really knowing less, rather than knowing more. Instead of being ready to hear God and live in His excellent ways, we settle for the immediate, instant gratification that never satisfies but only draws us deeper into confusion.

". . . and they knew that they both were naked" (Genesis 3:7a). She wanted to know so much and see so much, but now all of a sudden they are naked, *"And they sewed fig leaves together . . . and hid themselves from the presence of the Lord*

God. . . ." (Genesis 3:7b-8). After our mind has been activated and we become motivated and commit a sinful act, condemnation *automatically* comes and makes us want to hide in shame from God. The battle of the mind started in the garden of Eden. After God had so exquisitely, uniquely wonderfully and beautifully made the mind, then it became unsound.

In this case, Adam and Eve left the state of God-consciousness and entered into the state of self-consciousness, and forever afterwards their minds had to be fed externally to elevate them above the self-conscious state.

The mind is a terrible thing to waste. If you don't have the truth, which is the first knowledge, then all other knowledge doesn't mean a thing, because you are without a foundation. Foundation comes from the root word *fundus*, which means first. The Word is our first law, first rule, and first principle. If you do not first have the first laws as the foundation, you will hold on to any information as truth that is presented to you. If we sometimes feel as if we have a mind "like a sieve," we think that we can't *retain information*. Loss of memory and inability to hold facts so as to use them are effects of our mind having become unsound. This descent into chaos began with Adam and Eve, and we haven't stopped falling since.

So it is a terrible thing not to find your mind, or be able to "keep your wits about you." Irrational and illogical thinking plagues us so much that people turn to drugs, alcohol, and other things for mind stimulation, because they have no built-in resistance to pressure. People can't handle pressure, and so they run to alternative solutions to get themselves together. How are you going to get yourself together when you are spaced out? "I got to get something to drink; I've been sober too long." Does that sound like the product of a sound mind? Our solutions only create further problems; when are we going to remember to turn to our Creator who knows what we need?

Not knowing where to turn, we become "ceremoniously insane." Many of us Christians go through all the motions, but we are just as crazy as a bedbug. If you read some of the letters we get from people who say, "Pastor, I'm leaving because you have that American flag on the back wall." Or, "Pastor, I'm leaving because you have Christmas trees on the pulpit." You've got a Christmas tree in your house, knucklehead! I'm just being a little facetious, but you should hear the things that people leave the church for. And all they have to do is look around and say, "Look, Pastor, lust is burning me up. There's this guy I've got to go back to."

Individualism and independence have affected, and even become, the American religion. "I know God for myself. I don't need any man to teach me anything; God speaks to me now. I don't care what the elders say or the pastor says. I say to my soul, 'Do what you want to do. For Apostle Paul says that all things are lawful; all things are just not expedient. But right now it is expedient that I go with Joe Green's wife, that I go to bed with Jack Paluka's daughter.'" That's what believers say in their minds; they are *ceremoniously insane.*

Proverbs 16:25 says that there is a way that seems right to a man, but only brings him death. When you try to convince your own mind that wrong is right, God says you are a fool. Our folly will only cause our lives to be required from us. In other words, our own mind will place a demand on us that we are not capable of handling, and we are going to go insane.

If we think ourselves so prosperous that we don't need God or anyone else, a time may come that places tremendous demands on our intellect. Because of our lack of truth, the circumstances will overwhelm and blow our mind to oblivion. Institutions are currently full of people who couldn't handle the pressures of the world which placed unreasonable demands on their minds. And that's why a lot of Christians, as well as people in the world, lose their grip and go off the deep end. Do not lose your mind; renew it.

The rich young man in Matthew 19 kept all of the laws, but there was one thing he still lacked. Jesus told him to go and give to the poor what he prized most of all—his belongings. Before Jesus challenged him, he was sound minded in his own eyes. He said, "I've done all of that." Jesus told him to go one step further in order to build up lasting treasure in heaven. But the man's possessions had *him*: any time you don't want to follow the source that gave you the blessing, you're insane.

Success in life is based on accurate decisions made from reliable information—directly from the source. Many people are in harrowing situations because they made decisions governing their lives based on false information.

Let's look at the word *fool*. A fool is someone with little or no judgment, no common sense or wisdom. In other words, a fool is mentally deficient. When our lies come back to us, they will make a fool out of us, make us lose our credibility, and cause others to withdraw from our company. Satan lied to Eve and made a fool out of her. We buy into his lies to the point that we lie to ourselves and make fools out of ourselves. Self-deception is a great enemy to the mind: the devil doesn't have to work hard to keep those who lie like him.

A lie is very damaging if you believe it, and it occupies a place in your thought life where truth ought to be. A lie is also contagious: it will contaminate everyone with whom it comes in contact. If our light is darkness, how deep will that darkness be! (Matthew 6:23). If we prefer the deception of being able to do as we please to the exclusion of God's Word, we cannot experience the power of genuine spiritual liberation that truth brings into our lives. Jesus said in John 8:32 that *"You shall know the truth, and the truth shall make you free."* We have to be set free by the Son to be free indeed (John 8:36).

Because the carnal mind is enmity against God: for it is not subject to the law of God, neither indeed can be (Romans 8:7).

The carnal mind is against everything that God stands for. Before a man is born again and has his mind renewed, his mind is carnal, and is thus at odds with God. The word *carnal* means "in or of the flesh; materialistic or worldly; not spiritual; having to do with or preoccupied with bodily or sexual pleasures." As a result, the carnal mind has difficulty taking in the messages of the Spirit that feed the human spirit.

The word *enmity* denotes "a bitter attitude or feeling; hostility, antagonism; a strong settled feeling of hatred, whether displayed or latent." Some people in the world will show hostility when you talk about God. Even some Christians will get upset if you talk about God or try to live holy if it is a way that has not been revealed to them. Some of them harbor hostility, and pretend that they do not. Others will display their dissatisfaction with your beliefs quite readily—Christians and non-Christians alike.

It is important that after you become born again, you allow the Holy Spirit to redeem your soul or your mind.

Pure religion and undefiled before God and the Father is this, to visit the fatherless and widows in their affliction, and to keep himself unspotted from the world (James 1:27, emphasis added).

The Holy Spirit sets up a classroom in your mind; He trains you so that your mind can become renewed and redeveloped so that you can perceive the thoughts of God and can use it as an antidote for change. If you listen to Him, study the Word so that it can be engrafted or impregnated in you, and communicate with God, the Holy Spirit will keep your mind sound. And people won't be able to influence you to deviate. They won't be able to force you to compromise what God has revealed to you.

It is not that you are better than them; God has just made you more aware of how He sees things. He has given you a proper understanding of what sin is. We get a glimpse of how holy God is, and how far above our ways and thoughts He really does dwell. We are made aware that we need to strive to imitate Him more closely than we ever have before. Otherwise, how could we pray for others, when we feel so lost ourselves? We need the Savior to take back the inroads the deceiver has made into our minds, to give us sound minds (II Timothy 1:7).

Why is it that so many Christians are not happy? They don't believe the Word: God blesses them one day, and the next day they don't believe in Him any more. I have come to the conclusion, as a believer, that we must start believing in God and start living it. Because as long as we are in the mode of believing, there are some things that we are not going to believe. Why? Because they are going to get us out of our comfort zone. Church, you have to get your mind settled on this thing, because satan is going to come at it. He's going to come at your mind with all he's got to dissuade you from your purpose.

Remaining carnally minded leads to becoming a reprobate—unprincipled and depraved, those to whom Jesus' dying on the cross is rendered meaningless. When you are not of a sound mind, you are not a principled person, because Jesus is all about principles. You have to learn principles. The reason people walk around the church ceremoniously insane is because they don't have the principles operating in their lives. The word *unprincipled* means characterized by a lack of moral principles. The unprincipled mind is unscrupulous— without law, rule and truth. The soul of the mind is saved from day to day; it is a *continuous process*. You don't get smacked upside the head, and instantly you are saved for the rest of your life. The whole world might knock you down, but you have to get up and still have a sound mind for tomorrow. It's called *working out* your own soul's salvation—an experience of bringing the soul and the mind in line with the spirit and knowledge of God's Word. Redemption of the mind is progressive: you continue to work on it every day. The mind matters that much.

When you have your mind renewed, it will affect your whole being. When your mind is renewed, you just won't do things that will harm your body or your spirit.

The mind is not accustomed to the things of God. When your heart becomes changed—opened to receive the Lord's ways—and you attempt to change the pattern of your thought, your mind will fight you. You try to get so holy, and admit it: it's a battle. You tell the saints, "pray for me especially late in the night around 2:00, that's when I have my worse times. Call me—I'll be pacing the floor at that time of night. People, I need help. Somebody needs to be praying for me—this thing has got a hold on me. I'm trying to fight it, but I need some help." Stop acting like you are Charles Atlas—like you are one of the strongest men in the world; you don't know how to handle the devil. Whatever that problem, challenge or habit is, you need some help. Stop trying to be macho; get some help. You have been coming to the church for years, and still have bad habits. Seek help, because otherwise it will eventually uncover you to your shame.

Your mind feels it is under an attack, and it will come up with all kinds of excuses for you to leave it alone. It says, "Let's stay like we are." But God will stretch your mind, and once it is stretched, change will come.

Chapter Seven
The Mind Matters II

Ephesians 3:20 says that God's power working in us is able to do in us far greater things than we can ask for or fathom. We need to ask God for the things we need to make our calling successful in His eyes. II Corinthians 10:6 mentions that we want to have *"a readiness to revenge all disobedience, when our obedience is fulfilled."* A renewed mind is a mind that stays ready; it is a mind that stays prepared and developed so God can use it. More than this, the mind strives to attain holiness just as much as, and even more than it indulged in fleshly appetites. Once our minds have gotten a taste of the glory of God, we will want nothing else. Jesus, the "new Adam," repaired the breach caused by the first Adam, delivering those in bondage (see Hebrews 2:14). Therefore you must stay free by casting down those ideas that seek to bring you back into slavery.

When you understand that renewing the mind is not optional but necessary, then problems start minimizing themselves. We are a natural-minded people, but we must profess and live a spiritual and natural mind lifestyle, with the spiritual mindset in control, guiding and informing the natural mind. Grace perfects nature. Our faith is seeking understanding; theology teaches us to put the faith into terms we can understand so that we might keep it all the more faithfully.

The weapon of our warfare is a mental one; faith is a weapon of the mind. When we have sound minds, we can lay ahold of eternal truths and, when we put those truths into practice, we will have eternal life. Strongholds of negative, degrading and fearful thoughts can inhibit the activity of Christ in your life, whereas the Word of God can arrest your thoughts.

Reasoning is a man's way to live, but faith is God's way of life. We need to understand that God does not despise man's mind, for He created it. Until a Christian's mind has been renewed in the ways of God, it cannot think clearly. Since satan lied to us, all the way back in the garden, that lie has been perpetuated and promulgated all the way down through the history of man. Until we get our mind renewed with truth, the Word of God, we aren't rational. All of our reasoning becomes false or less than accurate when put up against the blinding brilliance of God's revelation. God calls to us, *"Friend, come up higher"* (Luke 14:10). Jesus is not running an elite social club; He wants everyone to be holy and perfect as He is (Matthew 5:48). He wants us to succeed and bends over backwards to show us it is possible. Jesus went "the extra mile," and stretched it infinitely to show us that what He did first, so shall we do.

The voice of the mind is reasoning; the voice of the body is feeling. Why? Because it is in touch with the natural realm. The voice of the body and the voice of the mind are influenced by the voices of environmental and external teachings, which are inspired by Satan, the father of lies. You are educated by that in which you grew up in. Science has spent millions of dollars to develop the physical part, and millions have also been spent developing man's intellectual process. If his spirit can be educated and improved, so can his mind be educated and improved. We put most of the emphasis on the spirit, and hardly put any emphasis on the mind. We spend time developing our muscles and toning them up, gaining or losing weight. We also spend a lot of time as believers praying about furthering the life of the inner man, but we do very little about the mind. Beloved, I want to tell you that the mind matters.

We human beings cannot understand spiritual things without a natural mind. But that mind must be elevated and transformed by God's power for us to fully understand the Word of God.

As an example, one important way we need to renew our minds has to do with racism, a sin in the Church. We are one in the Body of Christ, many members but one body. Do we still determine whether or not we are going to love one another based on our skin color? If we say, "Well, we don't see color," we lie, for we do. We see color, but it shouldn't matter; we should love one another regardless, because we have the nature of God, since all things have passed away, and have become new (II Corinthians 5:17). We cannot profess to be born-again believers without unconditionally loving every born-again believer of every creed and color. If we don't work within that type of mindset, we have lost our minds. James writes that if believers want to get their minds or souls saved, they must put aside all "naughtiness," and with meekness accept His saving Word, not only hearing but acting on His Word (James 1:21-22).

God saw the man He created, and said in Genesis 1:28 that he was good and should "be fruitful, multiply, and replenish, and take dominion." He said this command to every man. God has given us the ability to have dominion, and so we ought to take it. But He did not say, "take dominion over one another." He said, "over creation." So, if you feel that you are superior to another person, you have lost your mind.

Jesus said, *"I am the way, the truth, and the life"* (John 14:6); we are to follow Him by keeping His words and commandments. Jesus says that whoever does so, will be loved by the Father and the Son, that Jesus will "manifest" Himself to him, and that the Father and Son will "come unto him and make their abode with him" (John 14:21,23).

But you can't love and follow Him until you get His

mindset. He knew we couldn't do it of ourselves, so He sent the Spirit to remind us of all He said and to teach us what He meant (John 14:26). He came to elevate us to a higher living standard, but many of us want to hold on to the old mindset, and so we cannot reach the level where God wants to bring us.

The world will not sit idly by while we are reaching upward for holiness and integrity of mind. People will try to bring us down the moment we aspire for something better than we already have.

There are some simple guidelines to follow so as not to conform to what we see around us in the world, and to avoid losing the sound mind, God has worked with us so long to recreate. Our own fleshly appetites get stirred up when we see what others enjoy, when we are going through a period of spiritual dryness, and when we become dissatisfied with the conditions and circumstances in our lives. In order to combat our restlessness, first we should not place our self-worth in what we possess. Never see yourself in the light of what you possess. Your self-worth is about who you are, not what you have. Who you are is the only thing that is going to last when what you have deteriorates.

For a second bit of advice, do not covet the possessions of others, for our desires will cause us to misbehave or lose our minds. We will do surprising, outrageous and crazy things once we let our minds get outside of where God created us to be. You will start taking advantage of your neighbor; you will start to cheat, steal, and do things that are unnatural or bizarre.

A third nugget of wisdom is not to believe that the possession of things is the answer to happiness. "Be fruitful and multiply" doesn't always mean material prosperity; there is also spiritual and mental prosperity. We can come to know and love God more, and share our findings with others who could benefit from the truth that builds our well-being in every way.

Things will not make you happy; money will not make you happy. The only thing that will make you happy is relationships; they are designed to make you happy. That's why, in Ephesians 5:25, God says through Paul, "Husbands, love your wives," so that you will be happy. "Wives, submit yourself to your husbands" (Ephesians 5:22) was said for the same reason. "Man, give your life to me so you can be happy."

Relationships are essential, for no man is an island. Co-worker, obey those that rule over you. Management, do not lord your power over your people so that they become discouraged. Why? So you can be happy. Relationships are where human happiness or fellowship comes from. Why are so many couples unhappy? They don't have a right relationship with one another.

A fourth lesson worth its salt is to have no anxiousness for the things of this world. Anxiousness is the devil's weapon he uses to kill you. Many people die of anxiety. Patience is God's weapon to get you the things that you need. Let patience have its time; it works. Patience will receive; anxiousness will take away from you. Avoid losing your mind by keeping yourself in perfect peace.

A fifth principle is not to be carnally minded. The carnal mind is ever against God. It will lead you to sin and eventually to death. To be spiritually minded is to think like God and to keep your mind in line with the Word of God. His Word makes sense of otherwise endlessly senseless situations. His Word gives clarity in the midst of a maze of tangled thinking, in the fog of fuzzy and odd ideologies. He will lead us out of the confusion when we acknowledge Him in all our ways.

A sixth suggestion is not to keep your mind on the system of this world nor to rely on it. The systems of this world will always let you down. They are flawed, designed to fail. They are also designed to make you depend upon them. That's what's wrong with the Body of Christ: we depend too much on the world and its systems. God is our source. The systems of this world are self-centered; the systems of God are kingdom-centered, focused on the principles of God. If you become a believer, you are to opt out of the world's system and operate in the system of God.

But God hath chosen the foolish things of the world to confound the wise . . . And base things of the world to bring to naught things that are: that no flesh may glory in his presence. But of him are ye in Christ Jesus, who of God is made unto us wisdom, and righteousness, and sanctification, and redemption: that . . . he that glorieth, let him glory in the Lord (I Corinthians 1:27-31).

If you don't understand that God can use anybody, then you will never have the mindset that will allow him to use you. Until you can understand that who you are in Christ—not where you are from or what you have done—is what matters, you won't have anything to do with what God is calling you to do. If God's working with us was based on our faithfulness, He couldn't work with any of us. But He does desire that we improve our faithfulness in thought, belief and action so that others will want to work with us.

Set aside the mindset of degradation, condemnation and failure. Forget about who you thought you were, and see yourself through your renewed mind—what God said He would do with you in this body, in this life—for you, through you, and for others.

But the natural man receiveth not the things of the Spirit of God: for they are foolish unto him: neither can he know them, because they are spiritually discerned (I Corinthians 2:14).

The natural mind cannot spiritually discern the things of God. That's why we have hangups in the Body of Christ. We have falsified truth being taught. See, you can live a lie as well as tell one, and many believers are living a lie. They "walk the walk" and they "talk the talk," but they aren't *thinking the thought*. We don't want to just get by; we want to shine with the saints in our full spiritual inheritance.

"But he that is spiritual judges all things" (I Corinthians 2:15). He that is spiritual—that has been renewed in the spirit of his mind—judges all things and compares everything to the Word of God. Now, if you are of a sound mind and you are comparing everything you do and say to the truth, if you compare spiritual things with natural things and you line them up to see if they correspond—and if you have good discernment of spirits because of your renewed mind, then you can stay on track, because you will clearly see the narrow road you must take, and know what it takes to stay on it to the end.

You need to renew your mind by connecting yourself to the supernatural through immersing yourself in the Word of God. Our mind must take on the level of the supernatural. Most people in the Body of Christ are thinking only naturally. We need to think supernaturally. Our minds must be *over* matter—not bound to this material, natural or physical world. See, when you become bound to this world in your thinking, you are limited to what you can do for God on your own strength. Because if you are operating in the natural, God can't use you. You can only do for God when you are thinking on the supernatural plane. Our spirits are to be in touch and in line with the supernatural, because He took on our human life and nature so that we could take on His divine nature and share in His divine life.

Our spirit life is superior to the physical, natural and material life. We must not let our five senses dominate, because the senses constitute a lower level of living than supernatural or spiritual living. The spirit is the highest form of living, enclosed in the physical body, with the five senses that communicate to this physical world. While the spirit of man communicates to the Spirit of God in the supernatural world, it connects us back to God, our source. The physical or the material is the lowest form of living; the psychological or the mental is the middle level; and the spiritual is the highest level of living. We have to use our bodies and minds to buttress or lift up the spiritual design and plan of living.

Until we allow our minds to be renewed, we can reach no higher than the middle level of living. If we are fleshly or carnally minded, we will remain in the lowest level of life. If we do not seek to understand the higher things, but are content with lesser things, no progress will be made. We will not be able to discern spiritual things, and so our mind is not what it could be.

Be encouraged, and reach for the stars. Spread your wings and soar like an eagle; climb straight up, leaving behind everything and everyone that held you back. God knows what wonders you'll find, and find them you will. These are the components of a dream.

Fly right, and do not continue to do the unwise things that frightfully yank you down to earth, wreak havoc in your life, and cause you to become a statistic in the Body of Christ that gives God a bad name to the world. You'll be a hazard to the effectiveness of the church until you get your mind renewed, so start now.

Beloved, God can do nothing with a person who has an unsound mind. God discerned Cain's mindset because of his flagging confidence. He said to him, "Why has your countenance fallen?" (Genesis 4:6) Many believers are sad because they are of the mindset that God does not love them. The truth is He loves regardless of our response and even reaches out to us more when we are downcast. God blessed Abel and his offering because he gave Him "the firstlings of his flock and the fat thereof" (Genesis 4:4). God blessed his obedient heart, which put God first. He acted out of first principles. God likewise continues to bless everyone who walks in *obedience*.

Even Jesus was tempted until he heard what the Lord said. Thank God who lives in heaven and in my heart for not only did He take away the sins of the world, but He made Himself to be righteous so that we could be righteous. John had to baptize Him to fulfill all righteousness, and Jesus humbly submitted. He did it to show us how to *win*.

For who hath known the mind of the Lord, that he may instruct him? But we have the mind of Christ (I Corinthians 2:16).

Not only do we have the mind of Christ, but we also have the status of Christ. When we get the mind of Christ, we will be sitting in heavenly places. We are going to be above principalities and powers. Our feet are going to be dangling over all of the spiritual wickedness that hangs around the unheavenly places. We are going to be tempted, but we are going to be found without sin. The Bible says, "Many are the afflictions of the righteous, but the Lord will deliver them from them all." When we have a renewed mind, we have a delivered mind, and we have no fear or doubt in our heart. Why? Because Christ obeyed God. When we obey God, He will provide, deliver and protect us. But we can't obey Him until we get a renewed mind—that's what makes us willing and ready to make the necessary attitudinal adjustments and changes in behavior, as well as what positive actions to take. Jesus obeyed His Father's will that He must die on the cross. Therefore He prayed all night in the garden of Gethsemane to prepare Himself. God refreshed and strengthened Him in prayer, as well as prepared His mind to accept what was to come. His interior strength was what enabled Him to not shield his face from spittle nor refuse the hairs of His beard from being plucked. He even prayed for those who mocked Him and put Him to death. At the end, when every bit of His strength both moral and physical was exhausted, He said, "All is consummated," and commended His Spirit to His Father. Jesus is our example of obedience. His reward is eternal life to all who shall believe, beginning with the necessary renewal of their minds in order to get us to think as He thinks, and act according to His ways.

When we give over our minds to Him, our feet can be in the mud, but our mind and spirit will be in the heavens glorifying God. Our back can be against the wall, and yet we will praise our Messiah. We can be fretting on our job, and magnifying the King of Kings. We can have pains in our chest, and still offer a sacrifice of praise. The sea may be wide and the sea may be deep, but He can open the sea. The clouds may be dark, but He can bring light. They that are of a sound mind will see it. If His Word has spoken it, He is going to bring it to pass. He is going to perfect that which concerns us. The Bible says that He has begun a good work in us, and He shall bring it to completion. We've got to be of that mind, and not get weary of doing well. We will not be fainthearted or bail out; we will always be overcomers.

Chapter Eight
The Mind Matters III

You must always remember that believing is an act of our God-given will. Every man and woman has their own will, and believing is an act of that will. For just as people think in their hearts, so are they. We think of ourselves consciously, subconsciously, and with our conscience. The word *conscious* means aware of one's self as a thinking being, knowing what one is doing and why. Consciousness consists of normal mental activity. The word *subconscious* indicates occurring without conscious perception of the normal mental process and reaction. The subconscious is a controlled mental activity, from deep within a person. The word *conscience* denotes a knowledge or sense of right and wrong, and is known as the moral judgment that opposes the violation of a previously recognized ethical principle, and leads to feelings of shame if one violates such a principle.

> *But if our Gospel be hid, it is hid to them that are lost: in whom the god of this world has blinded the minds of them which believe not, lest the light of the glorious Gospel of Christ, who is the image of God, should shine unto them* (II Corinthians 4:3-4).

Many people in the world today are blind because satan—the god of this age and this world—has blinded their minds; therefore they don't understand others who live the born-again life. They can't understand when Christians say,

"God blessed me with this," because they are *self*-conscious and not *God*-conscious. Even believers that profess to be born again are not very God-conscious: they say they live the life of Jesus, yet they are still self-conscious or self-absorbed. Serious repercussions come from living self-consciously. Because people in this world are spiritually blind, they make fun of you when you tell them they need Jesus. When you tell other believers that they need more of Jesus, they can't believe it either. At one time, most of us couldn't see the need for Jesus, or the need to know Him better, because we were self-centered. But now the scales have fallen from our eyes, we have sought the Lord, and He is guiding us more closely than before—because *we* are seeking Him out (see Acts 9:8-9,18-22).

People who have been in the Church for a long time can retain spiritual "blindspots" because they are not aware of the areas in their lives that remain unsurrendered to the Lordship of Jesus. Their difficulty is one of perception: it is easier to accept Jesus as a brother than as their *Lord*. They profess belief, but do not give Him their whole hearts. That's why they tend to repeat the same mistakes, and stay in the same conditions for years. No matter what you teach them or preach to them, they desire to remain in the same state.

As humans, we don't want to change because we're comfortable as we are. But the Lord wishes we were either hot or cold, but not lukewarm (Revelations 3:15-16). If we took the same energy we put into our self-centered pursuits and use it to build up the kingdom, we could change the world. Paul had persecuted the Church with uncommon zeal; but with grace perfecting his nature, he became the greatest preacher and missionary in the world. Mary Magdalene was seized with seven devils (Luke 8:2), but was redeemed due to the greatness of her love for Christ (Luke 7:47), whose feet she washed with her tears, dried with her hair and anointed with costly perfume in preparation for His burial (Luke 7:38,44). It was she who was one of the few to accompany Jesus to the cross (John 19:25) and was honored with a personal visit from Him after His resurrection—the first recorded encounter with the Savior in the Gospels (John 20:16).

In the book of Exodus, the people could not hear Moses because they were angry and frustrated. Many believers today are likewise blinded by anger, frustration and anxiety. Let's release our unforgiveness, hatred and fear in order to make tremendous progress in our walks with God and glorify Him as Paul and Mary Magdalene did—with the witness of an extraordinarily faithful and fruitful life after our conversion. Let us make a complete break with the world and be sold out for Jesus.

It takes a sound and stable mindset to know God and to do the will of God. In James 1:8, we hear about a double-minded man. In Acts 17:11, the case is made for keeping a mind of readiness. Acts 20:19 and Colossians 3:12 write about the mind of humility—something we definitely need to know much more about. In Romans 1:28, the mind of a reprobate is mentioned. In II Corinthians 8:12, the Bible talks about a mind that is willing. In Ephesians 4:17, we hear of a mind that is vain; many Christians have vain minds. In II Timothy 1:7, the Bible talks about the mind of soundness. God has much to say about man's many mindsets. Having the right kind of mind really matters. More deserves to be said about the prosperity of the mind. In III John 2, it is written,

Beloved, I wish above all things that thou mayest prosper and be in health, even as thy soul (or your mind) *prospereth.*

In order to prosper mentally and spiritually, God must give us a revelation that we need in our spirit. We cannot understand spiritual things with a natural mind. Most people try to live their lives out of a natural mindset, but we can't do that because we try to reason out and rationalize everything and still don't understand all that we need to know. People say about the Bible, "I read it, but I can't understand it." They are reading it out of their intellect. We need to pray for an increase of faith so that we can get the message down into our spirits. When our "heart" is prepared and our mind opened to receive a communication from God, our spirit receives the revelation and illuminates the mind with that knowledge. The mind thus becomes conformed to truth, and reveals it to the senses and causes a change to come to the body—in short, we are made whole. This process is called salvation, which is continual and lifelong rather than instantaneous.

When your body starts craving to fill fleshly desires, you just say, "*Spirit* . . . do your thing," and the spirit will say, "*Mind* . . . do your job," and the mind says, "*Body* . . . obey." What did your spirit say to your mind? "Mind, listen: Your body is a temple of the Holy Ghost." And your mind said, "Body, behave yourself. You are the temple of God, and God wants to dwell in you more and more." That is how we are being made whole.

Eternal life is the nature of God received into our spirit to recreate us and make us a new creature by changing our nature. When our spirit man receives the life of the nature of God, it elevates us to a higher living standard, and that causes our mind to need elevation. There is a process that the mind must go through, because there is a *conscious* and a *subconscious*. The reconditioning or reprogramming of the mind must get into the subconscious.

The Word of God will condition your conscious mind for reprogramming the subconscious. God has designed us fearfully, wonderfully and uniquely with a conscious mind for what and how we purposely function. God has designed us with a subconscious mind that goes on automatic pilot to keep us alive. God has designed us also with a *conscience,* which is our developed value system that forms over a period of time. Your subconscious mind operates all the time to keep you automatically functioning in normal daily activities. Once your subconscious—the deep or the inner mind—is locked into any belief through learning or life experiences, it will not begin at once to respond any differently. So when Jesus said, *"You shall know the truth, and the truth shall make you free,"* He meant that it will make you free from your subconscious.

To reprogram your subconscious, you need to get new information or truth. Your subconscious is going to make decisions, whether you want it to or not, without you being consciously aware of it. For the last few minutes, you have not been aware of whether your feet were moving or remaining still. Your mind has not been on your feet, but your subconscious can make you respond. When your feet hurt, your subconscious can make you wiggle your feet so they become more comfortable.

Your subconscious sets boundaries and landmarks in your life which prevents you from going either below or above a certain level without rejecting it. Your subconscious functions from deep within, and will reject any change from normality to keep you in your comfort zone.

Meditation deals with the internal, the subconscious. The subconscious is like a gauge: it holds down growth and expansion, or holds back redevelopment and reprogramming of the mind. It wants to keep you in your comfort zone. It doesn't want you to do anything new, and it doesn't want you to stop doing what you are used to doing. But meditation can change all that: it can provide you with a spiritual experience on an on-going basis to allow your subconscious mind to lock into the new information. But it is a process which includes on-going changes that truly will affect your subconscious. You can't do it once and be done with it; you have to continue to do it until it affects your subconscious. That's why the Bible says, as you see the light, walk therein.

The subconscious is affected by repetition. You have to come and hear the Word often, again and again. Meditating by reading slowly and pondering over the inspired words of God will give you peace and set you at ease. God can do things in your subconscious when you are quiet and at rest.

Information is the difference between a lost mind and a sound mind. New information has the power to transform you, so you must change your comfort zone: set it above where you are now. That's why imagination is so important: it's the power or ability to go to a new place in God.

When you meditate on God's Word, you will elevate your comfort zone level to where God wants you to be. The Word will first change you, and then your circumstances will change. The Word will provide you with a spiritual experience on an on-going or repetitious basis that will cause your mind to lock into the new information.

In Acts 10, Peter had a problem with non-Jews, so God had to give him a spiritual experience to reprogram his subconscious. Traditionally Jews were taught not to associate with or mingle with non-Jews. Peter was prejudiced, but God wanted the household of Cornelius saved, because Cornelius was a devout man. He gave to the poor and supported the work of God, but he wasn't yet saved. Satan blinded Peter on this matter, and he needed to get rid of all those lies that ignorance had placed there. Lies need to be erased, and it only can be done through a spiritual experience. You have to get into the presence of God and hear what the Spirit is saying to the Church. In your deepest, innermost being, your mind has to be reprogrammed through a spiritual experience. You come to church to get into the Word and make it stay down deep. You need books, videos and cassettes to keep the Word before you.

God can cause the transformation of your lives through a spiritual experience. When you meditate on the Word of God, you elevate your comfort level to where God wants you to be. In a vision, there must be words preferably from the Bible. There must be images and visualization. There must be a reference from God as the ultimate authority. Also, surround yourself with pictures so that you can have a clearer vision.

What you see affects what you give birth to in your mind and imagination. Then God begins to do things, to show you things like he did Peter when he let down that sheet from the sky with all the "unclean" animals on it. The success of the mind and the thoughts directly corresponds the level of truth on the new information on which you have meditated.

Meditation has three components: verbalization, the things you say with your mouth; visualization, the things you see, or images and perceptions of the mind; and internalization, the things you discern in your spiritual perception. These are the three functional components for response to development for reprogramming your subconscious by meditation. Your mind will be a product of your environment, so you must be sure your environment is conducive to growth and development. Your life is a living expression for the uses of your mind and imagination; that's why you must maximize your mind.

My father left home at eight years old from South Carolina with nothing. The only education he had was third grade. He built seven homes with his own hands and raised oodles of kids—that's how many it seemed like in my house. We had four rooms, and it seemed to me like we had ten million people in there: everywhere you went, you were running into somebody. You had to do karate to get the second piece of chicken, but we never wanted for anything. When I was in high school, he built a brand new house. I later got a bachelor's degree, master's degree and doctorate; he had third grade education—but he maximized his mind.

Chapter Nine
The Mind Matters IV

I know the devil wanted my lovely wife to have somebody else, but he couldn't get her: I caught her when she was 13 to make sure. I crippled the opportunities. Yes sir, I babysat and rocked the cradle until she became old enough. Her father said, "Go away, she's not courting." The next Saturday, I was right back. Her father got up the nerve one Saturday night and said, "What are you doing back here? Didn't I tell you she's not courting?" "Yes, sir." I'd go out of the yard, but the next Saturday, I was right back. You have to be persistent when you want something. See, I knew she was to become my God-given wife when I first met her. When I went to the door of her cousin's house and they said, "This is my cousin from New York; she is moving back to Virginia." I said, "I'm going to marry you." I was only 15 years old, and I couldn't even spell "marriage." But I have her now, and she's all mine.

In the garden, Adam and Eve were in a perfect situation; everything was working to their good. But the enemy made them think that there was one thing lacking. God made man and said he was perfect and good, and now, all of a sudden, the enemy told them the opposite. When they swallowed that lie they became self-conscious. If you always dwell on yourself, you will always limit anything you attempt to do, because you are not your source. God is your source, and when you are plugged back into His strength, you are re-energized.

Before Adam and Eve disobeyed God, they were

God-conscious; but afterwards they became self-conscious. They began to rely on themselves as their source.

Until you plug into God, you have no viable ways, workable ideas or uplifting thoughts, because you are thinking only in terms of yourself. Every time there is a challenge, you see yourself as unable to measure up. So you have to keep your mind off yourself and stay God-conscious. I John 4:4 says, *"Greater is he that is in you, than he that is in the world."* It is not by my power or might, but by His Spirit.

God wants us to present our bodies as a living sacrifice, according to Romans 12:1-2. Ephesians 4:13 tells us to get our minds renewed and to conform to Jesus, or have the mind of Christ in order for us to be conscious of Him—our provider, our protection, our stimulation—and our desires are all caught up in our source, which is God.

We are three-dimensional. Our body is the third dimension of man. It is the one that houses our spirit and is composed of our soulish realm. And when you allow your body to control you, you are out of control, and your mind is lost. Many people are catering to their body, and their body has a boss called *feelings*. Because of sin, man no longer has access to God and His wisdom and knowledge; those things became secrets or mysteries to man. This life should not be a mystery. For God said, *"Eyes have not seen, neither ears heard, neither has the mind conceived, but it is revealed to us by his spirit"* (I Corinthians 2:9). If you are connected to God's Spirit in your spirit, then life is no secret to you. They that know their God shall be strong and do great exploits. Why? Because God has no secret that He will keep from you, and in fact, God has hidden secret things for you only—but only for those that are reconnected back to their source—God.

Satan stole Adam and Eve's relationship with God. They were created by, and spiritually related with God, in touch with Him. They knew, understood and respected God's voice. God said, "Adam," and he responded, "Over here, Father." He called to Eve, and she said, "Right here with him." Now, all of a sudden, God calls, "Adam . . . Adam. . . . Adam." They were hiding. "What are you doing, Adam?" "I'm hiding." "What are you hiding for?" Because he had disobeyed God. And believers today are hiding from the voice of God. That's why most of them don't like to come to church on Sunday because they know they are going to get a good whipping! See, church reminds you of your responsibilities, therefore, people become blame-casters. It started right there in the garden with Adam, "That woman you gave me." She responds, "The serpent." God says, "I didn't tell the serpent, and I didn't tell Eve. Adam, I told you." So, brothers, if it's not working in your house, it's not your wife, your daughter or even that knuckleheaded son of yours—because he wouldn't be selling drugs if you were the priest in your home. Instead of him getting high, he would be getting holy.

When man fell into Satan's trap, it allowed Satan to steal man's image, potential and visual perception of being like God. Most of you don't see yourself like God, and so you see yourself as incapable of being or doing anything different than what you have always done. Can you imagine the God we serve as seeing Himself as incapable of healing us? We ought to think like God thinks: all things are possible!

When man became self-conscious, he focused all of his attention on his soulish realm—intellect and emotion—and his body. We can still see that today with eating disorders, sexual addiction, drug addiction, alcohol addiction, and so on—it's all about self. You don't realize you're harming yourself, your neighbors, your husband, your wife and your families, because all you got your mind on is your self-gratification. But if your mind is on God, you will be helping other people.

The language of the mind is expressing life according to human reason. It rationalizes statistics and explains theories that solve no problems and give no solutions to the degradation and destruction of human relationships such as families, social groups, communities, economic units, occupational alliances and moral and spiritual relationships. The language of the body expresses what the body is feeling. The body has lustful desires to be fulfilled.

Galatians 5:16-21 talks about the works and the truths of the flesh: uncleanness, luridness, sorcery, envy, murder, selfish ambitions, etc. I John 2:16 talks about the lust of the flesh, the lust of the eyes and the pride of life. Man became so self-conscious or bodily conscious that both of them began to abuse themselves, one with another: men with men and women with women. That's what we are seeing today in the church: some churches are ordaining homosexuals and are marrying two men, and marrying two women. This was not heard of in the traditions of the elders. But because we have become self-conscious now, all we want to do is please folks and not please God. The Bible said where there is not faith, it is impossible to please God. Don't tell me those people are walking in faith when they are marrying those types of people that need deliverance; they are in denial.

Because that, when they knew God, they glorified him not as God, neither were thankful; but became vain in their imaginations, and their foolish heart was darkened (Romans 1:21).

They went from darkened minds to the minds of reprobates: hardened and rebellious. Satan deceived them into thinking of sex in ways God and nature never intended. Now they cover themselves with fig leaves. Today's culture produces all types of pornography, and even child pornography is gaining rapid acceptance—enough for the largest bookstore chain in America to sell it unashamedly. Videos are produced to help stimulate individuals. We need to study our Bibles, and talk with our wives about making love as a personal and spiritual thing that unites lovers in a mutual bond of unending charity—not solely to be used for pleasure as an end in itself. Man demeans himself and becomes denatured when he does not appropriate the virtues of God that are his inheritance as an adopted son of God.

Through man's self-consciousness, he began to see himself as his own god. Secular and atheistic humanism leaves no perception of a higher being, higher knowledge and godly wisdom. There is no one to answer to for the deeds of the body; no higher being to be accountable to. But every knee shall bow and every tongue shall confess that Jesus Christ is Lord. Are you God-conscious or self-conscious? Satan knows how to get at us, so he goes to great lengths to keep man's mind blind to the truth, by having him focus on self to the exclusion of God. Reasoning without faith is man's way to live; faith seeking understanding is God's way.

God made our minds because He wants us to use them. He placed in our minds a very important mechanism called the *imagination,* which gives us the power to go to a place without physically being there, to project a vision, then back up and begin already knowing the end because we can see it as a vision already fulfilled. That's how important the imagination is: in faith we can see what God is doing in our minds and lives and see His work as something we can count on, because God is faithful. We are learning to imitate Him, and it is important to visualize it in order to believe it is possible.

When man was created, God termed "good" everything about him, even his mind. He gave us the ability to think, imagine and to choose. The problem is that with man being self-conscious he would focus on self, the body, things of the natural realm, which can be seen, and man does not want to think any more. Thinking brings up disturbing questions that we do not want to face. Therefore, we fill our time with noise and activity so as to drown out the silence that unnerves us. Music has to be played non-stop, and the television is on for hours daily. As a result, when it comes to facing difficulties in life, we are more often *reacting out of our anger* and not *thinking clearly* to find a just solution. We do not want to be like wounded animals that strike out in self-defense. We want to be healed so that we can minister with the mind and heart of Christ.

Until a Christian's mind has been renewed in the truths of God, that person really cannot think clearly. God's revelation is what brings peace, clarity, discernment and direction. We need God to give us what we do not have in and of ourselves. Currently, over two-thirds of our teenagers have had sex at least once by their senior year in high school. They are trying to find themselves, to feel loved and express intimacy in the only way that has been presented to them as love. Teenagers are now also committing suicide at an alarming rate for no apparent reason. They have no bills, credit, taxes, etc. Some will say, "My girlfriend quit me." Are you going to jump off the bridge because your girlfriend left you—that would be killing yourself for somebody that doesn't even *want* you. Now you tell me that's good sound thinking. Some men find out their wives are going out on them, and they go and blow their own brains out. The lover has her all to himself now! He is glad you are out of the picture; now she's got your money and a new man. This shows how people are definitely not thinking with sound minds. Something isn't clicking here.

If you tried to live by the world's way, self-consciously operating in the flesh, the devil will keep you defeated and in bondage by winning the battle of your mind. Every time a battle comes up in your mind, the devil will win it because you can't battle with your own intellect. Your mind is not powerful enough, rooted enough nor experienced enough to handle the devil's devices. You need to live the Word of God and keep your mind focused on God.

If you are without God, you are nothing. "I don't need God." That's all right, but I better not hear you calling His name on your deathbed. Nobody needs God until the doctor says, "That's it"—*then* they send for the preacher. What preachers ought to start doing when they go to the hospital bed is this. When you say, "Preacher, would you pray for me? The doctor says I got 12 hours to live;" the preacher should reply, "All right, I'll pray for you. In the name of Jesus, I pray that the family will get you an expensive coffin, in Jesus' name. You rascal, you should have been in church when you were healthy."

The devil aims to keep you in poverty, sickness and disease—anything to keep you spiritually separated from God. His job is to keep as many men as possible blind and ignorant of the truth, which minimizes their potential to be fruitful and multiply in order to take *dominion.* Satan doesn't want you to fulfill the main thing for which God created you: to take dominion of the land or claim the spiritual authority to move in God's power and bring souls to salvation. Most people are walking around with the mind of the *dominated*, submissive to all the world's commands. Ignorance is man's greatest enemy. Most Christians are ignorant as to who they are, what they possess and the fact that God has a purpose for their lives; therefore, they live below their God-given privileges.

Let us make man in our image, after our likeness: and let them have dominion . . . over all the earth. . . . (Genesis 1:26).

Genesis 1:26 points to the need for us to take dominion. I John 4:4 says, *"Greater is he that is within me than he that is in the world."* We have delegated authority; the enemy should be under our feet in Christ. Cast out devils and lay hands on the sick, and they shall recover. The enemy can't bother me: he knows who I am and *whose* I am.

When you become God-conscious, you maximize your potential. The unconscious denial of conviction regarding forbidden acts or reality is called *repression*; you don't want to remember it. New ideas always tend to incite resistance. When you try to learn something new, you are going to resist it every time. Do not resist new ideas, because new ideas give you new horizons to conquer. Repression will provoke unconscious resistance. You won't even realize you are resisting it because it will be *unconscious*. Counter-resist with the ultimate mind renewal of meditation on the Word, and re-program and take back what the enemy has stolen.

Resistance is the act of resisting an opposing power. It retards, hinders, and opposes. Many Christians are in repression. The effects of the *unconscious* on human behavior reveal that there are drives, desires, attitudes, motivations and fantasies in one part of the mind of which we are not aware. You have some things up there in the back of your mind that you don't even know are there. Only the Word of God is going to get in there and drive that stuff out. The unconscious drives are important because without our realizing it, they are responsible for many of our conscious feelings, attitudes, and actions, and they influence our *relationships* with other people. The Word brings back to your consciousness the things which cause you to feel and react the way you do. You become aware of why you are feeling what you're feeling. You might think that you have no choice in the matter, but you really must be responsible for your own actions.

You know why a lot of people can't grow? They have things of their past that they can't turn loose. They have things in their minds that they can't put behind them. Paul said forget those things that are behind you and look forward to the things that are set before you (Philippians 3:13).

Genuine knowledge of truth is the product of what is immediately evidenced in the experience of the perceiver. The image a man has in and of himself stresses the internal forces to act out what he feels. But it doesn't always have to be that way. When you know you are made in the image of God, you become God-conscious, and the gates of hell shall not prevail against you. What are you thinking inside yourself? Defeat? Failure? Because what you think has everything to do with what you are going to be.

Neither can you deserve what God desires because you cannot prove what is good and what is the accepted will of God, because your mind is not on God. For this reason, we say that if your mind is not on God, you have lost it. Because God is your source, and when you are disconnected from your source, you cannot get replenished. The importance of a sound mind is that it is set on God—it is God-conscious—at all times. To behold the beatific vision of God—to behold Him face to face—is heaven itself. We need to see that He is what is *real* in life, and if we would be really real, we would stick close as a sheep to its beloved, unfailing Shepherd.

So the mind does matter, but it must be full of God. New ideas always tend to incite resistance. We must instill a new mindset in our minds: we desire to become all His, to place our mind in the mind of Christ, give Him our heart and will, and go where He leads us, for what He has for us is what we have hungered and thirsted for all our lives.

Chapter Ten
Mind Over Matters

Moreover thou shalt provide out of all the people able men, such as fear God, men of truth, hating covetousness; and place such over them, to be rulers of thousands. . . . And let them judge the people at all seasons: and it shall be, that every great matter they shall bring unto thee . . . so that it shall be easier for thyself, and they shall bear the burden with thee . . . then thou shall be able to endure, and all this people shall also go to their place in peace (Exodus 18:21-23).

There are great matters in people's lives. When these matters become great, they override our minds, and we need someone to come and minister to us because we are in trouble. When matters become too much for us, they supersede the established mind, leaving it unable to function properly; in other words, they are not in their right minds. Now when people's minds in the church are above matters, they can help the pastor bear the burden. But when matters are clouding over our minds, we become the burden.

We cannot endure until we have our minds ruling over the matters of life and are in a position to help those who have great matters to bear.

He that handleth a matter wisely shall find good: and whoso trusteth in the Lord, happy is he (Proverbs 16:20).

If you handle things wisely, your mind is ruling over those matters. But when your mind is weighed down by the matters—when matters have superseded and built up a stronghold—the matters are overseeing your mind, and your mind is of no use to you.

Psalms 45:1a says, *"My heart is inditing a good matter."* My heart is entertaining good things and is overflowing with joy. I am able to be of a sound mind, and my mind now is inviting good things to enter it. It is consumed in contemplating the things of God, *"speaking only of things which I have made, touching the King"* (Psalms 45:1b). The mind dwells on things concerning the King or provided by Him in the kingdom. So, when you become a king and a priest unto God, your mind should be filled with good things pertaining to the King who is in charge of the kingdom.

I beseech you therefore, brethren, by the mercies of God, that ye present your bodies a living sacrifice, holy, acceptable unto God, which is your reasonable service (Romans 12:1).

God is commanding you to present your body as a living sacrifice because there are laws operating in your body that, if you allow the matters of life to overpower your mind, then your mind will sign a contract with your body against God. And the Bible says that he who walks after the flesh cannot obey the things of the spirit.

Romans 12:2 says, *"And be not conformed to this world."* The body is in contact with this world. If you allow it to stay in contact with the world, it is going to influence your mind with the matters of life. *"But be ye transformed by the renewing of your mind."* When you come into the kingdom of God, you need your mind renewed, because your body will not deliver: it only *reacts* to its feelings, which are in touch with the reality of the world. When you become born again, only your spirit is made new; your body and your mind still have to be saved.

When you have the wrong thoughts, you will have the wrong imagination; when you have the wrong imagination, thoughts become strongholds, and eventually controlling strongholds, over your mind. You are controlled by the matters of life.

Be not conformed to this world *". . . that ye may prove what is that good, and acceptable, and perfect will of God."* Many members of the Body of Christ have never proved what is good and acceptable in the sight of God and what is the perfect will of God for their lives and for the Church. That's why the Church is so troubled and in need of revival.

Ephesians 4:23 says, *"And be renewed in the spirit of your mind."* In a mind that has not been renewed or elevated, the imagination will reflect that there is no fear of God in them. A runaway mind will imagine things that are not true. It will tell you things about another that are not true and have you thinking so harshly and damnably about another person that you won't go near them. They could be one of the most blessed sisters or brothers in the Body of Christ, but your mind is not renewed, so you don't allow your love to cover your thoughts. People's thoughts do not make them sinners: they reveal to you that they are carnal—not yet matured.

Proverbs 1:5 says, *"A wise man will hear, and will increase learning, and a man of understanding shall attain unto wise counsels."* But a fool will not hear with increased learning, for Proverbs 1:7 says, *"The fear of the Lord is the beginning of knowledge; but fools despise wisdom and instruction."* We have deprived Christianity of its reality when we say and do whatever we think. We don't fear God any more. Fear is the first principle; reverence for God is the beginning, and not the end, of knowledge. True wisdom is to justify God and to condemn self; but most of us condemn God and justify ourselves. There's a loss of respect for divine authority and God-given leadership because of what we think or the way we think things should be or how we think they should go, based solely on our limited understanding—what we have learned and accepted—as opposed to the whole picture. Our minds have become the arbiter of reality—now we decide what is and what is not. The Lord is set aside.

But you are only what you are, and know only what you know, by the grace of God. You only can do what you can do by the grace of God alone. *"For it is in him that we live, we move, and we have our being."* You can do nothing of yourself, so you have no room to boast. So you have to incarcerate any thoughts that derive from vain imaginations or strong arguments against the will of God.

In Romans 8:5-6, we see that people who live out of the flesh set their minds on the things of the flesh. When you do so, the matters of life control you. But the minds of those who are concerned with the things of the spirit are unaffected by turbulence and turmoil: they continue to function properly and peacefully under fire.

But without the Spirit, we can only walk around with things dying in our lives because we are carnally minded. We stay bored, depressed, troubled, confused and irritated. Everything and everyone and every thought gets on our nerves. But when we are spiritually minded, we walk in good life, health, peace and prosperity.

God's people become enemies to you when you think carnally, for you think people are after you or against you. *"For* [the carnal mind] *is not subject to the law...."* (Romans 8:7). It will not reference the law, or God. *"... neither in deed can be."* It has no capacity or ability to hear and obey God. You've got to get rid of a carnal mind; you can't operate with it.

If there be any power in your life by the Holy Ghost, any

praise, reverence or fear of God in you, meditate in your mind on the things of holiness (Philippians 4:8). These are what purifies and conditions your mind to be able to stay over the matters and concerns of life. Whenever your mind becomes burdened with trash, trash it and think on these things.

Esther 3:1-6 lets us know that we need never be intimidated by, or envious of, the prosperity of the wicked, for their days are short. Mordecai never got moved by Haman's promotion; he knew his stand and relationship with God. Though *"all the king's servants . . . reverenced Haman,"* Mordecai did not bow or bother with it; he did not worship the man. *"then was Haman full of wrath."* The world, and even some in the Church, will get mad at you because you are trying to be faithful to what God has taught you. Haman wanted to choke Mordecai, but found out he was a Jew and that all of the people in captivity were his people. So he resolved to destroy his whole race, just because Mordecai would not bow to him. Sometimes just because people can't have their way in the church, they want to kill the whole vision.

In Esther 4, when Mordecai realized that Haman had tricked the king into declaring to kill him and all of the Jews, he went into fasting. He never allowed the matters to override his mind; he just operated in biblical principles. When the fire was heated up, he stood on the Word and *"cried* [out] *. . . before the king's gate"* (Esther 4:1). He got closer to the enemy. When the devil is raging, fast and pray, and God will hear you by touching the hearts of those who are able to help you. In this way, Esther was at first grieving for matters that were overpowering her mind. Mordecai was fasting and praying, and believing in deliverance, but she was living in the king's quarters; she had it made.

And she sent raiment to clothe Mordecai, and to take away his sackcloth from him, but he received it not (Esther 4:4).

She wanted to stop him from practicing kingdom principles and serving God—things he was supposed to do. When matters start controlling your mind, you no longer want to do it the Bible's way; you want to do it the world's way—what you think is the easy way. Now she was a Jew; she knew she was supposed to go in sackcloth and ashes too. But she wasn't functioning well because she became distressed; her mind was bogged down.

Mordecai didn't receive the offer that she sent from her carnal mind. But the king put a contract out on Mordecai and all of the Jews. So Mordecai told Esther, "I want you to go before God with me on this matter." Esther had originally become queen because her father Mordecai received a revelation from God to enter her in the beauty contest. The power and favor of God were all over her, and she won the beauty contest (Esther 2:9). She replaced the former queen, who had displeased the king (Esther 1:11-12).

Mordecai wanted her to go before the king. The matters dealing with the Jews were so distressing to her that she no longer felt that she had to submit to it because of her position in the king's household. So she didn't really want to go before the king. She couldn't see the importance of the survival of the whole nation of Israel because she herself was blessed. But what she failed to realize was that she was a Jew. For the Bible said, "We rejoice with them that rejoice and mourn with those who mourn." When we get blessed, we don't want to give anything to the Church to help those who are not blessed. We have to remember those who have so much less than us and those who have nothing.

In verse 14, Mordecai told her that if her prosperity was not based on the Lord as her source, it would be fleeting. She then recovered her senses, fasted and set herself to seek an audience with the king. Her life was on the line if she was rejected, because she was Jewish as well. She got the fear of God in her, did what she was clearly led to do, and found favor (Esther 5:2).

This kingdom is not for you to have your way; it is for you to walk God's way and be blessed. When you start obeying the whole counsel of God's Word, you become prosperous (experience the fruits of your redemption), and you get peace of mind, direction and find yourself taking actions that benefit other people even unto their own salvation.

Chapter Eleven
The Right and Wrong Way of Thinking

In Isaiah 55:6-11, God talks about a way of thinking and even the level of thinking. The poorest man in the world is the man without a dream. The most frustrated man in the world is the man with a dream that never becomes a reality. The ability of children to dream is a natural, mental instinct. No matter how poor or rich we are, we all have childhood dreams. These dreams are visual manifestations of our purpose, seeds of our destiny, placed in the soul of our mind—the imagination. The imagination, which consists of contemplated thoughts determined by what we believe, makes it either possible or impossible to reach our destiny successfully. God must have created and given us the gift of imagination to provide us with a glimpse of our purpose and to activate the hidden abilities within each of us.

Right or sound thinking offers innovative solutions for the world's ever increasing problems. History shows that the value of life decreases and the quality of existence diminishes when a generation loses its ability to think from sound, creative minds. It causes people to lose their sense of destiny. Our people have lost their sense of destiny. There is no unity among nations, states, cities, communities and churches because our thinking is wrong. We have been taught independence, but we have overindulged in it. We baptized our mentality and now we have a nation where every state thinks independently, and every person thinks independently. But God created us as a corporate body, a nation to turn the heart of the people back to God the Father.

Many teach that the kingdom is not about positive thinking, but Jesus brought positive thinking to the earth. Negative thinking is what got us in the shape that we are in. The word *think* means to form or have in the mind, conceive, to hold in one's opinion, judge, consider, to resolve or work out. Think is a general word meaning exercising the mental faculties so as to form ideas, to arrive at conclusions. Look at the word *reasoning*: it is to think, to bring to mind, to form an idea, to recall or recollect; the use of the mind for arriving at conclusions; making decisions; to weigh something mentally. The word *reason* implies a logical sequence of thoughts starting with what is known or assumed and advancing to a definite conclusion.

Before God formed Jeremiah in the womb, He gave him instructions for his purpose and destiny on earth. From this, I want to show you how negative man thinks, even back then. "Before I formed thee . . . I knew thee" (Jeremiah 1:4-7). You have to understand that God sees man differently from the way man sees himself. When God formed us in the belly, there were preconceived, preordained, predestined things in us. And God knows that they are there, and He knows we are capable of being what He has made us to be. And when we say and do otherwise, that is negative.

"And before thou came forth out of the womb, I knew thee." Before you were even extracted from the womb, you rascal, I set you apart for this. What are you talking about? Can you imagine me going into General Motors and saying, "This car isn't running right: this engine should be behind the car, not in the front. The trunk should be up front. I've seen Volkswagens like that." Can you imagine that? That's what we try to do with God. Don't you think the manufacturer knows what He built in you? Can you imagine me telling the

Mercedes Benz people, "I can't run at 160." We got the horsepower and the know-how mechanically installed in us. Come on. Get on out there and do it! What we have in us could change a nation! But as long as we think negatively, it will lie dormant. No potential will be extracted from us; fear will put a cap on it. Fear comes by what you hear and say, because your confessions become a reality to you.

Exodus 3:10 says, *"Come now . . . out of Egypt."* God is so positive about Moses—an old runaway murderer. "Who am I," Moses said, "to speak for the people?" Who are we to build the Church? You think I am going to go and tell my mama that she needs Jesus . . . or my boss? Moses couldn't believe God wanted *him* to take the children of Israel out of bondage. We don't really trust in the deliverance of God, so we say we already have it and therefore don't need it. That's why we are not bold enough to tell others that God can deliver them. We're negative. We do not talk about healing because we don't really believe it or want to be healed; we want to be fine just the way we are. We say, "Aren't we even good enough for God?" But we can always get better. Why is there a need to change our thinking? Because there is some awesome work for us to do.

You can do whatever is on your heart. You are equipped and well able to possess the mountain. But you have to prepare your mind. You have to have a prepared mind. Brush aside all negativity. See what you *can* do, with the confidence and persistence of God. God has prepared incredible things for His people who are prepared to be blessed by believing in His power to do what He said He would. He takes pleasure in the prosperity of His people.

God is a God of order; everything that God does is done in an orderly manner. There is a logical coherence in the arrangement of physical elements sustained by the various laws.

The Bible reveals God's presentation of His spiritual order and provides a systematic plan of self-development.

The will of God is not dependent on your past experiences, but solely of what His Word says. God cannot bring His will to pass on the earth without human cooperation and participation. Throughout the Bible we see situation after situation where God seeks the aid of man to produce His will in the earth (see I Kings 17:9-16).

God cannot bring His will to pass in your life without your cooperation and participation. If the promises of God and visions God has placed in our hearts are to come to pass, it will require our wholehearted participation and effort.

Based on your capacity to believe and act on what you believe determines what is possible for you to accomplish in your life, in your family, in your finances and in your career.

Life is always choice-driven and never desire- or wish-driven. Your future is directly linked to the quality of choices you make.

The new birth is a transformation of your spirit. This experience opens the door for a relationship with God through Jesus Christ and an understanding of the principles of Scripture. Surrendering your life to the Lordship and leadership of the Lord Jesus will set in motion the plan of Godly success and destiny. From that moment, you must begin to make decisions in line with the principles and precepts of God's Word.

We make choices in life based on one of several influences. Either we make choices based on the lust of the flesh, the lust of the eye, the pride of life, the influences of public opinion, the influence of satanic counseling or the influence of the Word of God.

The teachings of and belief in the Word of God should have the most influence on our thought life. Making decisions based on the wisdom of the Word of God will always bring natural, emotional and spiritual success!

When you become a born-again Christian, you become part of the spiritual family or the kingdom of God, which is referred to as the family of God.

The problem is, you bring your old inferior thought pattern into the kingdom of God, which is for the most part contrary to the teachings of Godly principles. A mind that is void of the control of the ministry of the Holy Spirit with the Word of God is incapable of correctly directing your life.

The spiritual enemy of man, Lucifer or satan, has his method of hindering man and it is rarely with direct confrontation, but an assault on man's thought life. It is his desire to keep you locked into the old life, thinking and acting contrary to the thoughts of God for your life. It is his thought pattern that you once adopted and lived by before entering into the salvation covenant with God.

Incorrect thinking will cripple your decision-making. It will retard your faith and keep you from overcoming life's challenges. There is a right way and wrong way to think!

Decision-making is not solely based on the facts and information or opportunities at hand, but on how you have been trained to think and how you see yourself.

What you believe has a direct effect on how you see your self. How you see yourself will affect the quality of the decisions you make.

Because decision-making is so critical to success, you will experience a better life if you learn how to make better decisions.

There is a link between how you think, what you believe, the decisions you make and what you will accomplish in life. You must learn the power of mental decisions that you make in order to maximize your full potential and to bring glory to God.

Logical decisions trigger the supernatural power of God that will bring victory and change the course of your destiny. What you see is what you can be. People do what people see.

When you make a logical decision to do something in your life and with your life that will glorify God, you trigger the supernatural power of God and grace of God to bring it to pass.

"And we know that all things work together for good to them that love God, to them who are the called according to His purpose" (Romans 8:28). In a divine intervention, God will raise up somebody somewhere to use their power and influence to assist you in life.

In order to improve the quality of your decisions, you must change your way of thinking. III John 2 says, *"Beloved, I wish above all things that thou may prosper and be in health, even as thy soul prospereth* [develops or changes]." Ephesians 4:23 says, *". . . and be renewed in the spirit of your mind."* The functioning process of the mind must be changed.

The Bible strongly teaches the believer to work at renewing the mind. You are responsible for the development of and management of your thought life.

> *For though we walk in the flesh, we do not war after the flesh: for the weapons of our welfare are not carnal, but mighty through God to the pulling down of strong holds; casting down imaginations, and every high thing that exalteth itself against the knowledge of God , and bringing into captivity every thought to the obedience of Christ* (II Corinthians 10:3-5).

You are responsible for participating in the transformation process and ongoing maintenance of your thought life. This is a mandate and not an option. Regardless of what man says, he is what he thinks, according to Proverbs 23:7.

When the Bible speaks of renewing the mind, it is talking about the transformation of the decision-making process.

Seek ye the Lord while he may be found, call ye upon him while he is still near: let the wicked forsake his way, and the unrighteous man his thoughts: and let him return unto the Lord; and he will have mercy upon him; and to our God, for he will abundantly pardon. For my thoughts are not your thoughts, neither are your ways my ways, saith the Lord (Isaiah 55:6-8).

The new birth does not instantly change your behavior or thought process; that comes through the process of renewing the mind and conscious discipline. This is what most believers fail to do. This is what must be done in order to prove what is that good, and acceptable and perfect will of God, according to Romans 12:2.

From the teachings of the Bible, we understand that man is a tripartite, or three-fold or three-dimensional being. Man is a spirit being. He lives inside a physical body and possesses a soul. The Word of God is the only thing that can penetrate the three dimensions of man, according to Hebrews 4:12.

The soulish realm of man has five basic components: the mind, will, imagination, emotions and the intellect, The soul of man is what determines the unique personality, characteristics, attributes and traits of the person.

When you make Jesus the Lord of your life, you are in essence making the Word of God the Lord of your life. The will of God is revealed in His Word.

God works within His divine effectual power that He orchestrated to change or establish your thinking. Isaiah 55:8 says, *"man must forsake his ways and thoughts. . . ."* to be conformed to the mind of Christ.

In Philippians 4:8, the Bible encourages man to develop his mind based on Godly principles so that life could be lived to its fullest.

Let's take a look at the three mechanisms of the mental

capacity: (1) the conscious mind, (2) the subconscious mind and (3) the conscience mind. The three work together in a divine systematic order.

1. The Conscious Mind handles the present conscious thoughts and day-to-day decisions and the initial reasoning and logical thinking that require concentration and directive thinking.

2. The Subconscious Mind is the independent flow of cruise control of the conscious mind, which has the responsibility to carry out automatically the finished work of the conscious mind.

3. The Conscience Mind houses your belief and value systems. It is the statistical data context by which all things are judged, appraised or determined. It is the heart of the decision-making process, From here, all things are judged by a preconceived standard. As things occur in life, this standard of judgment is developed which now acts as a system of operations in the production of truth, whether the information is true or false.

When the conscious mind has thought through a process and has accepted certain norms and values as truth, from that moment on the subconscious begins to handle decision-making at a level which does not require much conscious thought at all.

God has equipped you with the subconscious mechanism which helps you carry out known tasks which have been purposely learned without much conscious thought. The subconscious assists the conscious mind and eliminates the necessity to rethink known tasks and values over and over again. This is powerful, but also dangerous because if what you believe is wrong, it still will become reality to you. Your perception is reality to you.

Your subconscious is very beneficial to keep you on track in life, determining if we are on the right or wrong course. It will access our beliefs and value systems at a non-conscious level all the time, which is a valuable asset. These are pre-arranged beliefs and values.

The process is an independent flow because with the assistance of the subconscious, after a process has been thought through and acted out, the next time when faced with the same or a similar situation, the subconscious takes over and handles the decision-making without much thought. When you sin or do good it is a contemplated action.

The subconscious accesses information in the conscience and makes decisions on an ongoing basis without much thought. When the conscious mind processes information, the logical or rational thought process and values are stored in the conscience to make its values, judgments or quality decisions.

To have a renewed mind is to function in accordance with a new value and belief system. Remember, Proverbs 23:7 says, *"As a man thinks in his heart, so is he."*

The conscience houses the values and beliefs that govern our lives. It is similar to stacking or storing information: the more we learn, the more is stored. The more we repetitiously say or do a thing, it becomes an experience and is learned and stored.

The subconscious has been divinely programmed by the Holy Spirit with the Word of God to go to this storehouse of information to make decisions and give directions to the body.

There are two storehouses in this conscience cavity: the knowledge and information received *before* meeting Christ and the knowledge and information received *after* meeting Christ.

All your life, your subconscious has always accessed information received before meeting Christ and this old information is what was believed to be the most reliable and a type of preconceived truth.

Even though after coming into a relationship with and knowledge of Christ, you have to continue to add Biblical information of proper behavior to the after-knowledge of Christ storehouse. This storehouse is not being accessed by the subconscious to automatically make decisions in agreement with it. This must be done or practiced purposely and it is done by being a doer and not just a hearer of the Word of God only.

In order to act in accordance with this new after-Christ information, it requires much conscious purposeful effort because the subconscious does not yet see this information as reliable and to be depended upon. In other words, the Gospel truth has not yet been proven reliable over the old information.

According to Joshua 1:8, mediation, confession or professing a doer of the Word is how you retrain your mind.

After much struggle, any mistakes, failures, trials and errors, finally the subconscious is retrained to access this information from the after-Christ section and it becomes easier to make righteous decisions. There is a divine order in which the mind can function; when properly understood, we can eliminate years of struggle and accelerate the renewal process.

When you effectively and systematically confess, profess and activate the Scriptures in our lives, it will retrain or reprogram or renew the function of the subconscious, so that it goes immediately to the after-Christ information storehouse.

If the conscience has not been properly trained and developed, it is wrong to "let your conscience be your guide."

The conscience is the belief system or value system that has been developed over time and its development has been influenced by four main factors which become the basis for your decision-making: your social environment, influential people or associates in your life, repetitious information and personal experiences.

Your social environment helps shape what you believe about the world around you. As you begin to develop mentally, the social environment imposes certain preconceived truths about life that affect the development of your value system. Man is a product of his environment. Whatever he is exposed to is what he learns. His perception of life is a product of his comprehension of his environment.

Influential associates teach you certain things about life and living that become a part of your conscience or value system—be they parents, relatives, teachers or ministers. Those we are told to respect and listen to affect how and what we choose to believe about life.

Your mind is designed to accept information that is fed to it on a consistent basis. Whatever you hear over and over and over eventually makes its way into your thought process and possibly your belief system.

The most potent impact on your belief system is your very own personal experiences. In order to change or transform the belief system or the conscience, which is the essence of the renewal of the mind, you must work within the framework of these four factors.

God mandates His people to do certain things to develop a God-centered thought life. Working within the environment principle, the Scripture encourages the believer to control his environment and keep company with those who are also Godly. You must discern those coming into your life. They can either take you under or take you over. People are a prophesy of your future.

The reciprocating principle of repetitious information, the Scripture encourages Biblical meditation, repetitious rehearsal of truth and a consistent prayer life.

There are three types of schooling experiences: a human experience, a soulish experience and a spiritual experience.

The components of a schooling experience are words, images and emotions. What are we saying, hearing, watching, feeling and doing? A human schooling experience is an event which actually occurs in your life. A soulish experience is an event which occurs in the arena of the mind, such as hypnosis, nightmares, dreams and things imagined. Note that a soulish imagination can be so real that like a human experience, it can affect your body in ways similar to a human experience.

A spiritual schooling experience is initiated by God through divine visions, or can be initiated through meditation. Meditation provides us with a spiritual experience on the canvas of our imagination that will make a potent impact on our value system, either changing or reinforcing what we believe. According to Ephesians 3:20, *"God is able to do exceedingly, abundantly above all we can ask or imagine, according to the power that worketh in us."*

Biblical meditation involves what any human schooling experience includes—words, images and emotions. The subconscious and conscience work together in the decision-making process to keep us on a safe course in life. When a soulish or spiritual schooling experience occurs repeatedly, the subconscious and conscience accept it as a real experience and make the necessary internal adjustments in the belief system and judgment process to keep us on the defined course.

Meditation is God's plan to accelerate the transformation of our mental capacity, renew your mind and incorporate new vision and vitality into your life.

Chapter Twelve
The Center Focus of Mind/ State of Being

Mental clarity and revelation gives us the knowledge that we have been given life-giving power and motivation to live purpose-driven lives, so that we can become the light of the world, the salt of the earth, the city that sits on the hill.

Your mind is a very important element of your existence. You need your mind focused in the right direction. I am saddened for many people in the Body of Christ because they are not taking heed of how important it is to protect their minds and their imaginations. The mental state of being is so important that Paul talks about it several times—in Romans 8 and 12, and Ephesians 4. You need to be conscious of your state of being at all times, for your life affects other people whether you know it or not. So do not be fearful; be an effective witness of faith.

Let not your heart be troubled: ye believe in God, believe also in me (John 14:1).

Do you understand that the redemptive works of Christ make us free from fear? Salvation is a package of completeness for the whole totality of being. Be mindful of the redemptive work of Christ: it is a creative force of God, predestined from the foundation of the world to destroy the works of the devil, so that you will no longer have to be intimidated by anything that he will bring to your imagination, if you happen to let it penetrate. Let not your heart be troubled.

Thou wilt keep him in perfect peace, whose mind is stayed on thee: because he trusteth in thee (Isaiah 26:3).

If your mind is staying on the Lord, He will keep you in undisturbed peace. You have to have a consciousness of God's divine omnipotent and omniscient power; you have to realize that He is all-powerful, all-knowing, and ever-present. You will have this state of mind if you trust Him and consciously meditate on Him. You can keep your mind on Him 24 hours a day, seven days a week, because you trust Him. You are consumed with His Word and His purpose for you.

In all thy ways acknowledge him, and he shall direct thy paths (Proverbs 3:6).

The center focus of your mind is on Him. Be conscious of Him at all times; keep Him before you in all your ways. You cannot lean on your own understanding; it will fool and deceive you because your five senses are in touch with this world. Protect your mind and your imagination. Satan will bring delusions to your mind; he will bring thoughts from without your mind, and you will think that they are your own thoughts. But you know who you are. Be conscious of God in you, and of you being in God. Focus on that relationship because if you do not, Satan will develop one with you in your mind. Remember, not everything that shines is gold.

Let's look at the word *intimidation,* because everything in this world is geared toward intimidating you. To intimidate is to make fearful, frighten, disturb, stalk, hinder, or to prevent you from having a blessed and abundant life. This is the way Satan works. If he can intimidate you, you can't dominate. That's why when a child is born, one of the first words he learns is "No" or "Leave it alone." He has the spirit of domination in him. You say, "Stop it," and he says, "No." Even when you discipline him, he still says, "No." Why? Because he is created to dominate.

But as he grows up, our society and culture drives out and minimizes that dominating spirit in him. He will become a person of dependency. People break the spirit of domination in you, and you become a person of dependency, a timid-minded person. Intimidation projects fear. Fear has a lasting effect so that you no longer need to be intimidated any longer, because now you are walking in fear. If you are fearful, you are no more of a problem to the enemy, for you will not do anything that will threaten his hold on you or everyone around you. If you do attempt something, he will exploit your weakness so that people turn against you and your work goes up in smoke. For no one respects a weak, fearful person; they will take advantage of you, getting away with as much as you let them. Their urge to dominate surfaces.

Fear, alarm and agitation caused by expectations or revelation of danger will cripple you. If he doesn't want you to benefit from something, he's going to generate fear in your heart for it. What could help you the most—things such as developing a relationship with a key person of faith or attending a retreat that could change your mindset and life—will become the worst and last thing in the world you'd initiate because of fear.

You have to have a stable mindset. Say, "I am blessed going in and going out. I'm the head and not the tail; I'm courageous; I'm bold. I'm victorious; I'm more than a conqueror; I'm on top of the world. I have a piece of the rock; I'm walking in domination; I'm walking in abundance."

Chapter Thirteen
The Power of Thought

The power of thought is so great that not only you but other people, as well, gravitate and respond to your thoughts, as does God, the angels and demons.

Let's look at the word *power*. It is the ability to do, act or produce; a specific ability or faculty; the ability to affect strongly; the ability to control others; authority; sway; influence; legal ability or authority; a person or thing having great influence, force, or authority. Let's look at the word *thought*. It is the act or process of thinking, reflection; meditation, cogitation; the power of reasoning; conceiving ideas; capacity for thinking; intellect and imagination. So then, let's put power and thought together. As a result of your thinking, you get ideas, concepts and opinions. Consider others with respect to your thoughts because you form ideas, concepts and opinions, and these can either help or hurt others. The power of your thoughts can affect you as well, because it reveals your ways and how you will treat other people.

Thoughts have power to produce ideas, concepts and opinions, having great influence, force and authority to affect other people. Look at the word *reflection*: the fixing of the mind on some subject, a serious thought or idea or conclusion. Examine the word *meditation:* continual thought or sound reflection on sacred matters. Notice the word *cogitation*: to think seriously and deeply about, or to consider. Thoughts have the power to produce concepts, opinions and ideas that have the power to affect the way people act, react and respond. Opinions, concepts, and ideas produce the reality of how a person thinks. Thoughts have the power to produce from reflection, meditation and cogitation, reasoning concepts that influence the imagination, which fixes the mind on a serious conclusion. They become strongholds, and they will have an effect on other people.

The power of thought can destroy you depending on what you are thinking—you, everyone, and everything around you. The power of thoughts is such that just one unhappy thought you have about your job is enough to make you unhappy. No one is bothering you; you get paid every week, but just that one negative thought has enough power to make you unhappy. Some people who are unemployed would love to get your job, and take less pay than you receive to get it. Brothers, others would just love to have that wife that you can't stand. Sisters, others would love to have your husband. Many times we lose husbands or wives by the power of our thoughts. You can negatively think about your spouse and drive them away from you while you are living in the same house. Some men's thoughts are so far from considering the importance of their wife, until there are actually no emotions or love left—all because of their negative thinking about their woman.

Sometimes you can get hurt in a relationship and take that hurt with you into several other relationships, and never give anyone an opportunity to experience the power of grace and love that is supposed to be part of a relationship. Through meditating, cogitating and reflecting you can develop a thought that is so powerful that it will literally cause you to self-destruct. Many people are self-destructing because of unforgiveness, revenge, hatred and bitterness. These things will destroy you from within. You hug and kiss and have sex, and you still literally hate one another. You come to church and act saved, and you walk around in church literally hating one another for some little discrepancy. You can't move on and get along because of the power of a thought; you have been offended and held onto the offense.

Many of us, because of the power of thought, have a tendency to think more highly of ourselves than we ought to do. We think highly of ourselves based on what we believe are our limitations, as if we couldn't get any better. God gave us all that knowledge, those skills, that charm and good looks. The only thing we can claim as our own is our sin. Everything good that we have comes from God.

We think about ourselves so much until we don't even consider God. We think that we were born with the supernatural powers of God in our lives. Many times we think so highly of ourselves that we forget that there is another power working from within us. So we have a tendency to not be successful because we think more highly of ourselves than we ought to. In order to feel good about ourselves we say that to do more is impossible. We put more emphasis on our limitations than we do on God's exaltation through His Son Jesus. But Jesus gave all He had on the cross, which is much more than we'll ever be able to give. Realizing that we are not the Supreme Being is the beginning of acquiring honest, good sense.

Chapter Fourteen
The Imagination of the Mind

For the earth which drinketh in the rain that cometh oft upon it, and bringeth forth herbs meet for them by whom it is dressed, receiveth blessing from God (Hebrews 6:7).

We need God to bring us to that level of knowledge where we can receive His thoughts. He gives us His refreshing rains to bathe us in prayerful peace and serenity so that we can take in His revelations and receive His blessings. We need to cultivate our lives by nourishing this word in our hearts.

But that which beareth thorns and briers is rejected, and is nigh unto cursing; whose end is to be burned (Hebrews 6:8).

When you are not cultivating your lives with truth, your fruits are going to be like thistles, briars and thorns. When most of us buy land, we clean all that off and burn it up.

But, beloved, we are persuaded better things of you, and things that accompany salvation (Hebrews 6:9).

That's what God wants of you and for you—the good things—and those things that accompany salvation. Many of us are taught about salvation, but are not taught about the things that *accompany* salvation. God works within the framework of our belief system to get us to accept what is already true about us: to accept His truth about who we are and to change our low self-image.

In my job, God raised me up and I don't know why. Don't ask me why, but He wants me to serve Him, and I always had a poor self-image. Why in the world would He raise me up to help others' self-image? I had problems; I couldn't see myself going to school, pastoring and so on. We all have to get to a point where we decide we can do anything we set out to do, for we are God's man and God's woman. Made in His image, we can do anything we can imagine. Believe in faith and imagine it well enough, and it will be impossible that we *not* do it. Assimilate this information into your belief system. *Assimilate* means to absolve or to incorporate into one's thinking. Change your thinking by assimilating the right information.

A *belief* is a conscious, organized, pre-established, perception of things by which all other information is judged. All that you hear and learn will be valuable once this new information is properly assimilated and applied. Declare all old, non-beneficial information as unimportant, unreliable and inaccessible to your thought processes. When you receive new information and you know it's true, then let old non-reliable information be gone. We assimilate things into our belief system through significant events that we experience, for bad and good. Concentrate on the good, and let the negative ones go.

> *When I consider thy heavens, the work of thy fingers, the moon and the stars, which thou hast ordained; What is man, that thou art mindful of him? and the son of man, that thou visiteth him?* (Psalms 8:3-4).

What is man that God thinks about him and has him on

His heart all the time? God made man in His likeness, and God just loves man. God has not forgotten you. But when you aren't operating in principles and precepts, you don't have the right things activated. Your lay-away is still in heaven; He has it already laid up for you, but you have to work first to get it. God is watching you; He has His eyes on you; He cares about you.

"And the son of man . . . thou visiteth him." Not only is God's mind on you, He visits you. There are situations going on in your life that are visitations of God—not the devil. Sometimes God shows up in a situation, and you think it's the devil because it's not what you want. Many times God is trying to get your attention, so He has to show up as something that is uncomfortable, unethical, unprincipled, not planned as you planned. God is trying to get our attention, saying, "Hey! I got something for you. Come on over here. Come on . . . come on." The only way He can get you over there is to allow something uncomfortable to shake you out of your comfort zone.

In order to help the prophet Elijah to get to the widow at Zarephath, He had to dry up the brook. He will dry up everything you planned in order to get you back where He wants you if you've veered off the path, or to get you to a new place in Him once you're ready. When you start going where He wants you, things will start falling into place. You can tell when you are out faith, because things don't work. You won't be satisfied; it won't fulfill your ego; it won't please your drive. It is not the devil: it's just God letting you know you are out of place. When I walked through a casino, I felt out of place. I heard all that money going ching, ching, ching. I knew I was out of place.

God did not complete creation, based on providing all the natural manifested things needed for man's existence. In order to perform as humans to fulfill our purpose and to reach destiny, we must look to the spiritual realm. What we need for our completion is still in the spirit realm, stored up for those who love God and are called according to His purpose.

With all of the God-given natural resources in conjunction with man's imagination, along with knowing the purpose and will of God, there is still much more that needs to be created and manifested, such as building schools, businesses, etc. God did not build a Wal-Mart; he planted trees. And we took trees and used our imagination to build Wal-Mart stores. We took our imagination and came up with the corporation. God did not create the shopping mall; He created the garden. We took the trees out of the garden and built the shopping mall. God was sitting there looking.

"No, Pastor, if we did it, then God did it." Nimrod built the Tower of Babel; God didn't build it. God went in and stopped them from finishing it. God is not necessarily involved in everything man is doing. God was the only one who could stop the tower. He wouldn't stop the physical work, for that would override the people's wills, and He has given us free will so that we would freely choose Him and His ways. So God only stopped the communication at the tower.

Man's imagination is critical to his ability to carry out any of his desires, and especially the divine mandate to subdue and manage the earth. The Hebrew word for *subdued* can be translated into "to be overcome through intelligent means." That's what I'm trying to get you to do: through intelligent means, you must overcome the ghetto mentality of living in poverty. Our imagination is at the very heart of our creativity and ingenuity. You are not a genius until you use your imagination. If you are not using your imagination, you are wasting a gift from God. Creativity is our God-given nature, bursting out of our imagination. You have pre-programmed, pre-destined things hidden and stored in your imagination. Only the truth can rattle your brains enough to prime you to think about it. That's why, when God went to Jeremiah, He said, "What did you say, man? You can't do what? Don't say that. I knew you before you were formed. Your assignment was given to you before you were placed in your mother's womb." In other words, God is saying: "I've got to go down here and get this man's imagination going." Your problem is not with the white man, the black man, or your job: it's the lack of imagination.

What does your imagination see? "Well, Pastor, I'm just taking it one day at a time." He who fails to plan, plans to fail. What are your imaginative thoughts? What are you dreaming about? "I don't know, I just want to make it to heaven." If you aren't resourceful, you aren't going to make it, for it takes everything you've got to make it—including your imagination. You have to have an imagination about how heaven is going to be; that's what makes you want to go there. The world doesn't want to go to heaven because people don't have an imagination for it. They say, "I'm in hell here." They *are.* We can create a level of hell here, but do nothing to improve it, such as giving our lives to the Lord.

> *And the Lord said, Behold, the people is one, and they have all one language; and this they begin to do: and now nothing will be restrained from them, which they have imagined to do* (Genesis 11:6).

Nimrod and company were building the Tower of Babel. It was not God's idea, but Nimrod was a master builder. We don't know that we too are builders. What are you dreaming of? A bigger apartment, or your first home? What is in your imagination? Another good used car? Dare to set your sights higher in faith.

Man's power and ability are unlimited in his imagination. When you realize your potential and the power of imagination, you will realize that you are unlimited and unstoppable. God said nothing on earth could stop Nimrod and his company. The only way he could be stopped was for God to come down and deal with it Himself. Building the tower was such a powerful and organized movement, so structured in communication, so sound in economics that they had all they needed to build it. They had all the money they needed to finance it and all the labor it took to build it. They stopped when God came in and confounded their language (Genesis 11:7).

So powerful and important is the imagination to men that God only altered their communication while they were building the tower, but he didn't lessen or destroy their imagination. Communication makes the difference as to whether you will be a people or not. When God confounded the language, they had to split up. God said they were dispersed all over the world (Genesis 11:8). Because when you can no longer understand one another, you are no longer unified.

Meditation affects the imagination. What are you meditating on? Whatever it is, it is going to eventually affect your imagination. Stop thinking about negative things and negative people; think about positive things and people who are positive. You say, "Well, there is only one person here." Well, take that one and meditate on him or her so that together you get the job done. Make the most with what you've got. Say, "Pastor, we can get it done." You might only be talking about two, but you are still saying "we."

Biblical meditation involves what any natural experience involves: words, images and emotions. Anything that you meditate on is going to involve words that have been said to you, or that you have spoken yourself. It's going to deal with images that you have seen, and with your emotions. So if you strive on negative things, it is going to effect your emotions, the words that come out of your mouth, the words that you hear—positive or negative. When you always think negative, and you hear something positive, you reject it. You can be around so many negative people that when positive people come around, you reject them.

The very person that I am trying to help is often the very one that gives me the worst problem. I'm a positive person: I believe in progress and success, and I won't accept anything else. When I talk with people, some of them reject me because they say I'm too positive. How can you be too positive? But you *can* be too negative. They hate to see me coming. "Oh Lord, look who's coming. Yes sir, Mr. Positive." "Boy, you are blessed man." "Boy, you look like a Rolls Royce." Some people say you look stupid and nappy-headed. Let your response to that be, "Well, you look like a Rolls Royce to me." You want somebody around you who is positive because your imagination is what's going to get you out of it, or keep you in it.

Meditation is God's plan to accelerate the transformation process to renew our minds, and to incorporate new vision and vitality in our lives for imaginable creativity. If you aren't creative, you're hurting. Renewing the mind can be accomplished by spiritual acts of meditation. In Psalms 1:8, it says, *"meditate day and night."* Meditation is encouraged throughout the Bible. God's people are instructed to meditate on the Word. Meditation is a God-given method whereby you can take the truth of God's Word and envision it having come to pass in your life, situations, circumstances, or events. Take the Word of God and hear God say, "I'm going to bless you." You have to take that word and see it come to pass in your life; then you won't want for anything. You have to take that and make that imagination manifest in your life. Then He will supply all of your needs. You have to envision yourself possessing the land.

Genesis 17:1-9 says that God promised to make Abraham exceedingly fruitful based on his participation and cooperation, and also his capacity to believe he was who God said he was, and he could do what God said he would do. Now are you participating with God, or are you fighting against truth?

One key to your performance is your self-image. If you positively change your self-image, you will raise your level of performance. Now God supernaturally delivered them from Egyptian bondage and brought them out under Moses to the promised land. It was there at the borders of the promised land that they had to make a decision to possess this land or remain in the wilderness.

We are at the border now, and it's decision-making time. What will we do? Most of us have come out of a bad experience—a bad past—and we have an inferiority complex. We think everybody is better and more suitable and more qualified than us. If we are going to succeed, our attitude has to be, "There isn't anyone living that is better than us or more qualified. He has equipped and qualified us. What we do not yet know, we can learn on the job.

Don't let fear of failure stop the work of the Lord from proceeding. God has not given us the spirit of fear, but of love, power and a sound mind. He has not said we would fail. So if God didn't give that idea to you, who did? The devil. So you need to turn around and give it right back to him. Changing how we view ourselves will considerably increase our ability to make quality decisions that will positively affect our lives and the lives of others around us.

In Genesis 13:14, Abraham came out of Egypt very rich. He had many servants and livestock, he was wealthy, and so was Lot. They were both so prosperous, and the land was so big that they actually had to separate.

God was training Abraham to cooperate with His plan for his life. God carefully instructed Abraham how to proceed and to possess the promise. "I want you to look at the stars. I want you to walk through the land—north, south, east and west. I want you to really see it. If you see it, Abraham, you can have it." You have to see what God has promised you in your imagination. God is teaching Abraham how to use his imagination. We all need to participate and cooperate with God's plan for our lives.

So God said, "Consider the stars. Can you count them? That's how blessed you are going to be. Look at the sand. Can you count the grains? No. Well, you aren't going to be able to count your blessings either." God told him to change his name from Abram to Abraham. Names denote nature. Abram's new name, "Abraham," means, "Father of the largest nation of people." God named him "Father of Ham's people." Abra-ham was rightly named because Ham was the son of Noah, and Ham had more descendants than anyone else at that time. Your spirit knows the meaning of your name, even if you don't know it. Every time your spirit hears your name called, your spirit responds to the nature of that name. That's why when God called a lot of people in the Bible, he changed their names. Abram to Abraham. You need to be positive; use your imagination. The imagination is crucial to our ability to carry out any desire, especially the divine mandate to subdue and manage the earth, which God has left totally in our control.

Remember meditation affects our imagination, so remember to meditate on the right things. Meditation is God's plan to accelerate the transformation process to renew our minds and incorporate new visions. It doesn't stop there; you need a new vitality, too. See, a new vision without vitality means nothing. We need new vision and vitality in our lives for imaginable creativity.

God is saying, "Whatever you can see yourself walking in, I'll give it to you." But Abraham had to know that what he wanted was what God wanted for him. If we want only to do His will, to be in the center of His will, we will not be ultimately led astray. What is in the center of God's will for us will make us the most happy—that's why He designed it that way. See how carefully God had to teach Abraham how to receive and possess the promise. All he told him was: walk to it; look at it, and see yourself with it. He had to meditate and imagine how it would take place based on the word God had spoken to him.

Now, according to Romans 4:17, *"Abraham was calling those things that were not as though they were."* He brought his desire into the realm of experiential imagination because God had instructed him to do so. That's what you need to do. Take your imagination and develop an experience of a thing before you get it. You need an experiential, spiritual, imaginable experience of the thing before you can get it. You've got to imagine such a vivid mental picture of it that it's so real to you, it's so much yours, so much into your possession that you say it's yours and you don't even have it yet.

And we desire that every one of you do shew the same diligence of hope unto the end (Hebrews 6:11).

Do not become sluggish, discouraged, bewildered, fainthearted, doubtful, *"but imitate those who through faith and patience have inherited the promise"* (Hebrews 6:12). Don't get envious, mad, bitter, angry or frustrated; don't start seeing them as better than you are—just follow their example of hard work done from the heart with the inspiration of truth in your mind.

Chapter Fifteen
The Endurance of the Mind

Wherefore seeing we also are encompassed with so great cloud of witnesses, let us lay aside every weight, and the sin which doth so easily beset us, and let us run with patience the race that is before us (Hebrews 12:1).

For you have need of patience, that, after ye have done the will of God, ye might receive the promise (Hebrews 10:36).

That the mind matters is possibly the most life-changing and revolutionizing teaching you will hear during your lifetime. The greatest battle that is waged against believers are fought in the cavities of the mind, and it is regulated and constantly repeated with each thought pattern. Every person is either an initiator or a reactor when it comes to the use of the mind in decision-making. The enemy tries to wage war with you in your mind because he knows that your decisions are formulated and calculated based on information and data that you have been given and received. The battle becomes drawn out as you grow older in the things of God. But the more you learn about the things of God, the greater the resistance you will encounter from the enemy, but the easier and the sweeter the victory will become.

Often the little things in life trip us up because they take integrity. We need mind transformation—mind transferral from the world to the kingdom of light. When Paul was called to preach the Gospel, he shared his testimony, saying that he wanted to call people from darkness to light and from the power of satan to the power of God, so that they may have forgiveness of sin. In order for us to develop integrity of mind, we have to have endurance of mind during these games that the enemy plays with us, which we call *spiritual warfare.* It takes integrity—the state of being complete in the mind—to make quality decisions.

Our system of values is so much a part of us that we cannot separate it from ourselves. It becomes the navigating system that guides us. It establishes priorities in our lives and determines what we will accept or reject. So the enemy plays a mind game with us based on our experiences before we gained knowledge of Christ. If he irritates us enough, he figures that we will reflect back to what we had before, hoping to get us to make decisions that are not sound and quality oriented—based on the Scripture. He attempts to cause us to miss the mark, or get out of the blessing plan of God.

He also works on our difficulties accepting some parts of the Gospel, like tithing and assembling ourselves together each week. We are all faced with conflicting desires, sitting right there in the church. No one, no matter how spiritual, can avoid this battle of the mind. It is going to happen every day of your life. Integrity is the factor that determines which one will prevail: you or the enemy. We struggle daily with decisions between what we want to do and what we ought to do. Many times we lose out to what we want to do, even if it is not necessarily what God would like us to do at the time.

Romans 8:2 talks about the law of the spirit of life, which is in Christ Jesus. In the law of the spirit of life, there is a principle called the principle of *recognition.* One of the greatest things that we can use for the renewing and the elevation of our mind is to recognize the intersection of the spirit and the mind, to recognize their function, which is lined up with the

Word of God. Recognize the intersection of knowledge and understanding, which produces wisdom. Recognize the intersection of mentor and protégé for perfection for instruction, rebuking and direction. Recognize the intersection of the spiritual and the natural; knowing how to operate in both realms at the same time because of Abraham's declared righteousness which we have inherited. Recognize the intersection of prosperity and wealth, understanding that God takes pleasure in prospering His people. And as we become wealthy, He warned the rich to be sure to disperse the wealth equally among those that have need, and make sure they are responsible in taking care of their family and the ministry.

You should have a great fear of *believing a lie* because you have to make quality decisions. Jesus said, *"You shall know the truth and the truth shall make you free"* (John 8:32). Our problems are created by *ignorance*. And the decisions we make were made, most of the time, based on ignorance. You can track every problem to something that you did not know, or someone around you did not know, so you had to base your decision on ignorance. All of us should have a craving for wisdom. You need wisdom, but you especially need Godly wisdom.

God's Word is like a telescope that looks over into the spirit realm that explains and shows us what's there for us. That's why you need to know the Word of God.

Proverbs 18:21 says that your words can bring your thoughts captive and control your behavior. With the wisdom of God's Word operating in your heart, and formulating through meditation in your mind, you can receive the word which will keep your thoughts captivated. How can you think the wrong thoughts when you are confessing truth? When you are speaking the Word of God, it's hard for you to think negatively or irreverently. So your words can control your thoughts.

Look at the word *endure*—it means to hold under, to stand, to bow, to undergo, to put up, to continue in existence. Look at the word *endurance,* and it is the ability to last, the ability to stand pain, stress, and fatigue. Romans 6:17-18 says to obey the Word of God from your heart, and He will free you from sin and make you servants of righteousness.

Romans 7:25 says, *"So then with the mind I myself serve the law of God."* So you obey the Word of God from your heart, and you serve the law of God with your mind. That's why the mind is important. You can't just get born again and keep that old unsound, unhealthy, unstable mind. We all want to get caught up in the praise and worship, and we all want the gifts of the Spirit, and we all expect the greatness of God to function in our midst, but our minds are not functioning properly.

We must be reborn in the spirit, but our mind must be renewed and kept sound with ongoing development and maintenance. Why? Because there are times when things can slip into our thought patterns. Mind renewal will make the difference between serving God and not serving Him.

But the only one who can help you regulate your thoughts is God, the source of our complete rest, perfect peace, and divine wisdom.

He restoreth my soul: he leadeth me in the paths of righteousness for his name's sake (Psalms 23:3).

The Lord restores our soul and our mind. But it is left up to the individual for maintenance and development of its soundness. *"My brethren count it all joy when ye fall into divers temptations"* (James 1:2). Count it joy when your mind gets tested and tried, *"Knowing this, that the trying of your faith produces patience"* (James 1:3). All it is going to do is produce patience. *"But let patience have her perfect work, that ye may be perfect and entire, wanting nothing"* (James 1:4).

For whatsoever things were written aforetime were written for our learning, that we through patience and comfort of the scriptures might have hope (Romans 15:4).

When you endure, you can have hope, because that's perseverance. II Timothy 2:3 says, *"Thou therefore endure hardness, as a good soldier of Jesus Christ."* You must always be ready for a good fight for the thought process. You have to be ready to defend your mind from the fiery darts of the enemy. You've got to fight to watch over your mind and your thought process, because your decisions will determine where you are going in life. Your attitude will determine how high you will go.

II Timothy 2:4 says, *"No man that warreth entangleth himself with the affairs of this life; that he may please him who hath chosen him to be a soldier."* You are responsible for the ongoing maintenance of keeping your mind sound after you have it initially renewed; it's up to you to get it *elevated*. You can't allow the cares of this life or opposition of the enemy to get your thoughts away from God's purpose or will for your life. You can lose focus on your assignment on the earth if you allow your environment or other external influences to hinder your soundness of thought for upholding clarity, sensitivity and passion for fulfilling the work for the kingdom of God.

II Timothy 2:12 says, *"If we suffer, we shall also reign with Him."* Reign with Him in a higher level of thought and actions.

Other books by Dr. Jerry Kelly:

Freedom, The Spirit of Liberty
The term, "servant of the people," is lip service only to many in leadership both in political and Church circles. In the Garden of Eden, God gave man the freedom to take dominion. Today, many Church leaders are still slaves to some form of bondage. As you read *Freedom, The Spirit of Liberty*, you will learn how to be truly free. As the Body of Christ walks in the spirit of liberty together, we will take dominion over the evil of this present age.
ISBN 0-927936-72-0 $8.99   124 pages

Image Ability & Focus
Image Ability and Focus will inform, enlighten, transform and renew your mind to God's Word. Prepare yourself for an exciting journey of information and inspiration of how to denote your image, ability and focus.
ISBN 0-927936-49-6 $8.99   112 pages

To order these books, write or call:
Antioch Christian Center
1800 East Washington St.
Petersburg, VA 23803
(804) 732-1998
(800) 268-7594

Destiny Image New Releases

GOD'S FAVORITE HOUSE
by Tommy Tenney.
The burning desire of your heart can be fulfilled. God is looking for people just like you. He is a Lover in search of a people who will love Him in return. He is far more interested in you than He is interested in a building. He would hush all of Heaven's hosts to listen to your voice raised in heartfelt love songs to Him. This book will show you how to build a house of worship within, fulfilling your heart's desire and His!
ISBN 0-7684-2043-1

THE GOD CHASERS
(Best-selling **Destiny Image** book)
by Tommy Tenney.
There are those so hungry, so desperate for His presence, that they become consumed with finding Him. Their longing for Him moves them to do what they would otherwise never do: Chase God. But what does it really mean to chase God? Can He be "caught"? Is there an end to the thirsting of man's soul for Him? Meet Tommy Tenney—God chaser. Join him in his search for God. Follow him as he ignores the maze of religious tradition and finds himself, not chasing God, but to his utter amazement, caught by the One he had chased.
ISBN 0-7684-2016-4

GOD CHASERS DAILY MEDITATION & PERSONAL JOURNAL
by Tommy Tenney.
Does your heart yearn to have an intimate relationship with your Lord? Perhaps you long to draw closer to your heavenly Father, but you don't know how or where to start. This *Daily Meditation & Personal Journal* will help you begin a journey that will change your life. As you read and journal, you'll find your spirit running to meet Him with a desire and fervor you've never before experienced. Let your heart hunger propel you into the chase of your life…after God!
ISBN 0-7684-2040-7

Available at your local Christian bookstore.

Internet: http://www.reapernet.com

Other *Destiny Image titles* you will enjoy reading

THE MARTYRS' TORCH
by Bruce Porter.
In every age of history, darkness has threatened to extinguish the light. But also in every age of history, heroes and heroines of the faith rose up to hold high the torch of their testimony—witnesses to the truth of the gospel of Jesus Christ. On a fateful spring day at Columbine High, others lifted up their torches and joined the crimson path of the martyrs' way. We cannot forget their sacrifice. A call is sounding forth from Heaven: "Who will take up the martyrs' torch which fell from these faithful hands?" Will you?
ISBN 0-7684-2046-6

THE RADICAL CHURCH
by Bryn Jones.
The world of the apostles and the world of today may look a lot different, but there is one thing that has not changed: the need for a radical Church in a degenerate society. We still need a church, a body of people, who will bring a hard-hitting, totally unfamiliar message: Jesus has come to set us free! Bryn Jones of Ansty, Coventry, United Kingdom, an apostolic leader to numerous churches across the world, will challenge your view of what church is and what it is not. Be prepared to learn afresh of the Church that Jesus Christ is building today!
ISBN 0-7684-2022-9

A DIVINE CONFRONTATION
by Graham Cooke.
The Church is in a season of profound change. The process is sometimes so bewildering and painful that we don't know which way is up or down! Here's a book that separates truth from feelings and explains the elements involved in transition. Its prophetic revelation and deep insight will challenge your "church" mind-sets and give your heart much food for thought. This book is a must-read for all who want to know what is happening in the Church today!
ISBN 0-7684-2039-3

Available at your local Christian bookstore.

Internet: http://www.reapernet.com

Other *Destiny Image titles* you will enjoy reading

MANHOOD GOD'S STYLE
by Rev. Wilbur Conway.
Society is hurting for true men—God's style of men—who, with Jesus as their example, are willing to accept responsibility and serve faithfully in their families, churches, and communities as priest, provider, and protector. These are men of integrity, holiness, wisdom, prayer, the Word, and the Spirit. Here Wilbur Conway challenges men of God to rise up and set the standard for true manhood—God's style!
ISBN 1-56043-318-3

DIGGING THE WELLS OF REVIVAL
by Lou Engle.
Did you know that just beneath your feet are deep wells of revival? God is calling us today to unstop the wells and reclaim the spiritual inheritance of our nation, declares Lou Engle. As part of the pastoral staff at Harvest Rock Church and founder of its "24-Hour House of Prayer," he has experienced firsthand the importance of knowing and praying over our spiritual heritage. Let's renew covenant with God, reclaim our glorious roots, and believe for the greatest revival the world has ever known!
ISBN 0-7684-2015-6

WOMAN, THOU ART LOOSED!
by T.D. Jakes.
This book offers healing to hurting single mothers, insecure women, and battered wives; and hope to abused girls and women in crisis! Hurting women around the nation—and those who minister to them—are devouring the compassionate truths in Bishop T.D. Jakes' *Woman, Thou Art Loosed!*
ISBN 1-56043-100-8

THE PROVERBS 31 WOMAN
by E.R. Reid.
The Proverbs 31 Woman focuses on the characteristics and roles of this godly woman and provides insights for both men and women today. It does not teach according to the world's wisdom but by the Word of God. This queen's perspective of a godly woman reveals that God's children need royal characters in order to be fit for His royal mates.
ISBN 1-56043-612-3

Available at your local Christian bookstore.

Internet: http://www.reapernet.com

Other *Destiny Image titles* you will enjoy reading

AN INVITATION TO FRIENDSHIP: From the Father's Heart, Volume 2
by Charles Slagle.
Our God is a Father whose heart longs for His children to sit and talk with Him in fellowship and oneness. This second volume of intimate letters from the Father to you, His child, reveals His passion, dreams, and love for you. As you read them, you will find yourself drawn ever closer within the circle of His embrace. The touch of His presence will change your life forever!
ISBN 0-7684-2013-X

FROM THE FATHER'S HEART
by Charles Slagle.
This is a beautiful look at the true heart of your heavenly Father. Through these sensitive selections that include short love notes, letters, and prophetic words from God to His children, you will develop the kind of closeness and intimacy with the loving Father that you have always longed for. From words of encouragement and inspiration to words of gentle correction, each letter addresses times that we all experience. For those who diligently seek God, you will recognize Him in these pages.
ISBN 0-914903-82-9

POWER TO SOAR
by Charles Slagle.
With this special pocket book you can enjoy personal notes from the Father's heart every day of the year. Although these lines are short, they have an impact that breathes encouragement into your life...and will almost always make you smile!
ISBN 1-56043-101-6

THE LOST PASSIONS OF JESUS
by Donald L. Milam, Jr.
What motivated Jesus to pursue the cross? What inner strength kept His feet on the path laid before Him? Time and tradition have muted the Church's knowledge of the passions that burned in Jesus' heart, but if we want to—if we dare to—we can still seek those same passions. Learn from a close look at Jesus' own life and words and from the writings of other dedicated followers the passions that enflamed the Son of God and changed the world forever!
ISBN 0-9677402-0-7

Available at your local Christian bookstore.

Internet: http://www.reapernet.com